LUCY SUMMERS runs her own successful landscape design partnership, the Open Garden Company, which has b̶̶̶̶̶̶̶̶̶̶̶ international clients. As an RHS-qualified horticultura̶̶̶̶̶̶̶̶̶̶ show gardens at the Chelsea Flower Show and has b̶̶̶̶̶̶̶̶ much-coveted Gold and Silver medals for her garde̶̶̶̶. contributes regularly to gardening publications, gives lectures to gardening clubs and organisations, and co-hosted *Britain's Best Back Gardens* for ITV among other television work. She lives in Surrey.

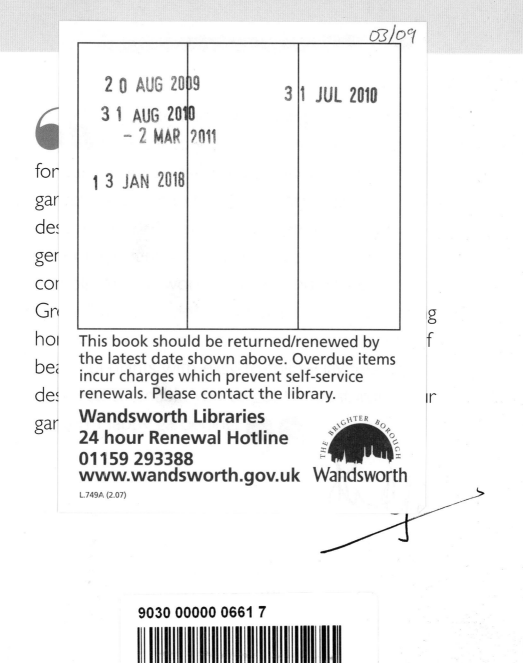

GREENFINGERS GUIDES

CLIMBERS AND WALL SHRUBS

LUCY SUMMERS

headline

Copyright © Hort Couture 2009
Photographs © Garden World Images Ltd
except *Holboellia coriacea* (p.18) © Andrea Jones and
Calystegia hederacea 'Flore Pleno' (p. 30) © Visions

The right of Lucy Summers to be identified as the Author
of the Work has been asserted by her in accordance with
the Copyright, Designs and Patents Act 1988.

First published in 2009
by HEADLINE PUBLISHING GROUP

1

Lucy Summers would be happy to hear from readers
with their comments on the book at the following
e-mail address: lucy@greenfingersguides.co.uk

The Greenfingers Guides series concept was originated
by Lucy Summers and Darley Anderson

A CIP catalogue record for this title is available from
the British Library

ISBN 978 0 7553 1758 5

Design by Isobel Gillan
Printed and bound in Italy by Canale & C.S.p.A.

Headline's policy is to use papers that are natural,
renewable and recyclable products and made from wood
grown in sustainable forests. The logging and
manufacturing processes are expected to conform to the
environmental regulations of the country of origin.

HEADLINE PUBLISHING GROUP
An Hachette Livre UK Company
338 Euston Road
London NW1 3BH

www.headline.co.uk
www.hachettelivre.co.uk
www.greenfingersguides.co.uk
www.theopengardencompany.co.uk

PICTURE CREDITS
All photographs supplied by Garden World Images

ACKNOWLEDGEMENTS
My thanks to Darling, Zoe, Serena, Lorraine, Emma, Josh,
Charlotte, Christine and Isobel. Thanks also to Michael
Loftus of Woottens Plants, Wenhaston. And to all my
wonderful nearest and dearest.

OTHER TITLES IN THE GREENFINGERS GUIDES SERIES:

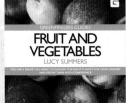

Drought-Tolerant Plants
ISBN 978 0 7553 1759 2

Fruit and Vegetables
ISBN 978 0 7553 1761 5

Contents

Introduction

ABOVE *Passiflora caerulea* OPPOSITE Wisteria and clematis

Climbers are, quite simply, glorious plants. Their kaleidoscopic colours, fragrant flowers, gorgeous leaf shapes and occasionally weird and wonderful berries and seed heads make them appealing in every way. Once you discover them you will find them totally addictive: a scented climbing rose is a heavenly aphrodisiac, and the drift of sweet jasmine in dusky twilight will fill the passionate heart with joy.

Climbers require little maintenance and are so gratifyingly easy to grow that you could actually fill a garden with them and precious little else. They do exactly as they say on the pot – they climb, and they are damned good at it. A well-placed climbing rose can bring a pastoral touch to a town garden and many of the fragrant choices, such as jasmine, will add a sense of the exotic to a modest suburban residence or even the smallest courtyard garden. Climbers will happily scramble over trellis or clamber up trees and that dark, damp spot where nothing else will grow could be an ideal position for a climbing hydrangea or ivy. Even dull, straggly hedges can be transformed by the introduction of a fragrant, rambling honeysuckle, and climbers are spectacularly effective for covering eyesores such as ugly walls, old sheds, garages and outhouses.

Garden spaces planted with climbers provide a delightful habitat by encouraging bees, butterflies and pollinating insects into the garden space. There is nothing more enchanting than watching whirling butterflies and dozy bees, intoxicated with pollen, spinning lazily through the flower borders on a summer's evening. If you ever happen across a wall of ivy in autumn thrumming with earnest bees, it sounds for all the world like a humming, vibrant apartment block. Wildlife in the garden adds an unexpected, delightful dimension.

Climbing plants really come into their own in urban areas where space is limited: gardeners can employ climbers to huge advantage by filling their vertical spaces as well as horizontal ones. In a small city garden, every plant needs to earn its place. In larger gardens, climbers are the glorious gilding on the lily. They are stunning when planted imaginatively with trees, shrubs or perennials.

Don't limit yourself to choosing climbers for their flowers; there is enormous diversity and seasonal interest in climbing plants, offering fragrance, architectural leaf shapes and wonderful berries and fruits. In fact, they tick just about every box a gardener could wish for. Please, please, I entreat you, take a risk or two – don't choose plants that sound 'safe'. Climbers are spectacular and lavish, so – apart from checking their suitability to your intended space – let yourself loose on a sumptuous plant adventure. Extravagance is the name of the game: choose wildly, unrestrainedly, and be as whimsical as you like.

Choosing climbers

What climbers you choose to grow and how you team them up with other garden trees and shrubs is largely down to personal preference. Ask yourself a few basic questions and you will enjoy great success in your planting exploits.

As a starting point, consider your garden's style. What colours do you prefer: gentle pastels or bold exotics? Do you want an informal or formal appearance? Do you want a scented climber? Or would you love to have a scrambling clematis to enhance an existing, perfumed climbing rose? Maybe you have neither of these yet, but have always longed for such a romantic pairing. Never be afraid of trying out your own combinations: what pleases one gardener may prove jarring to another, and following your own creative instincts will probably be eminently more pleasing to you than copying suggestions you read in a book.

Before you decide which climber to buy, think, too, about what you want from it. What job do you want it to perform? Do you need something to liven up a dull, unexciting wall, an evergreen screen for winter, flower screens in summer, or just additional colour? Does it need to hide an unsightly area, or have attractive seed heads to make the garden more interesting in autumn? These are all important questions, but, even more importantly, ask yourself how big the space is in which you intend to plant it and how good is your garden soil?

The garden's aspect is another important point to consider when choosing plants that will thrive there: does it face north, east, south or west? Does it enjoy sun all day long, or are some areas in shade in the morning and sunny in the afternoon? North-facing gardens are notorious for shade, perhaps only receiving a couple of hours of sunlight a day. Perhaps the garden is overlooked by large trees and buildings and is in shade nearly all day. It's imperative you gauge the amount of light in the garden and choose suitable plants accordingly. If you have a sunny garden, the range of climbing plants that will grow there is going to be greater than for a garden that is plunged into deep shade for most of the day.

You will also have to consider the region in which you live. If you have very fierce, bitter winters, you really need a tough old climber that can withstand cold and frosts. You may live by the coast, and there you would be wise to select a climber that is tolerant of salt-laden winds and exposed windy conditions.

If you take all these factors into account, you won't be tempted into impulse-buying a plant that isn't happy in its allotted space or, worse still, proves a potential nuisance in your garden. This is especially important in smaller gardens, where space is at a premium. You will have noticed that garden centres position anything that is in flower in a brightly coloured pot right at the front entrance, so as to tempt you into a spontaneous purchase. Resist! It is imperative you get your money's worth and buy a plant that really earns its keep. Too few gardeners give much thought to what they really need from a plant. You would hardly buy a sofa without thinking about the dimensions of the furniture or the space you have available in the house, yet plants are often purchased on just such a whim.

Last, but not least, how much time do you have to look after your garden? Perhaps you need to choose something that requires minimal pruning and very little personal effort or maintenance because you are just too busy doing other things to give much time to gardening. By considering these details you are bound to find a climber that ticks all the right boxes.

Because of the huge variety of climbing plants available nowadays, you will certainly find something in the following pages that will inspire you and will thrive happily in your own garden. This book outlines some of the most popular climbers and a smattering of those that are a little more unusual. Most of the suggested plants are easy to grow and widely available from good garden centres, mail-order catalogues and nurseries, so you shouldn't have too much difficulty finding something that pleases you and suits your garden situation.

Early-flowering *Rosa banksiae* 'Lutea'

Using this book

Each climbing plant listed is categorised according to season and its eventual height, with useful, practical cultivation advice that will encourage you to grow with ever greater enjoyment, creativity and confidence. More detailed information, covering all the different elements mentioned in the profiles, and including help with planting, pruning and propagation, will be found after the plant profiles. Lists of plants for specific purposes can be found at the back of the book.

Throughout the book, plants are arranged seasonally, but in practice the corresponding months will vary according to local weather patterns, regional differences and the effects of climate change. Additionally, the flowering times of many plants span more than one season. The seasons given are based in this country, and should be thought of as a flexible guide.

Latin names have been given for all the plants in this book because these are the names that are universally used when describing plants; the Latin name should be recognised by the garden centre, and with any luck you will be sold the right plant. Common names have also been given, but these vary from country to country, and even within a country, and a plant may not be recognised by its common name.

Skill level is indicated by one of three ratings:
EASY, MEDIUM or **TRICKY**

Many of the plants chosen for this book have been given the Award of Garden Merit (AGM) by the Royal Horticultural Society (RHS). This is a really useful pointer in helping you decide which plants to buy. The AGM is intended to be of practical value to the ordinary gardener, and plants that merit the award are the cream of the crop. The RHS are continually assessing new plant cultivars and you can be sure that any plant with an AGM will:

- be easily available to the buying public
- be easy to grow and care for
- be not particularly susceptible to pests or disease
- have excellent decorative features
- be robust and healthy

Early spring	March	Early autumn	September
Mid-spring	April	Mid-autumn	October
Late spring	May	Late autumn	November
Early summer	June	Early winter	December
Mid-summer	July	Mid-winter	January
Late summer	August	Late winter	February

SPRING

Early spring is my favourite time of year in the garden. Life begins to stir: young shoots peep shyly through the soil, bulbs emerge from their earthy burrows into splendid flower, the days are a little brighter and warmer, once-bare winter trees are tinted green as new leaf buds begin to shoot, and all around there is the promise of another exciting gardening year. The bulk of garden plants have not yet fulfilled their blooming potential, but the anticipation of all that is to come fills the gardener with hopeful expectancy. There are so many wonderful climbing plants that put on a good display in spring, and if you happen to be a fair-weather gardener, only bothering with summer-flowering species, you are really missing out on one of the most magical times of the year.

Ceanothus 'Italian Skies'

↑ 1.5m/5ft ↔ 2.5m/8ft   **EASY**

One of an indispensable group of evergreen shrubs that adapts well to being grown on walls, C. 'Italian Skies' has small, glossy, evergreen leaves and a profusion of the richest blue flowers in late spring to early summer. Ceanothus are reliable and beautiful in flower.

BEST USES Handsome growing up small pillars, low fences and walls, and invaluable for framing doors; makes attractive ground cover on a sunny, sloping bank, and ideal for sheltered coastal gardens

FLOWERS May to June

SCENTED No

ASPECT South, east or west facing, in a sheltered position; full sun

SOIL Any humus-rich, moist, fertile, well-drained soil

HARDINESS Frost hardy at temperatures down to -5°C/23°F; protect with a mulch or fleece in winter

DROUGHT TOLERANCE Excellent, once established

PROBLEMS None

PRUNING Cut out dead and overcrowded growth in late winter

PROPAGATION Sow seed in late winter; heeled softwood cuttings from late spring to mid-summer; semi-ripe cuttings from mid-summer to late autumn; hardwood cuttings from late autumn to later winter; root cuttings in autumn

GREENFINGER TIP *If you have dirty hands after a bout of weeding, rub a handful of flowers into your hands with a little water: they make a natural soap!*

Chaenomeles speciosa 'Geisha Girl' ⚇
Japanese flowering quince

⬆ 1.5m/5ft ⬌ 1.5m/5ft   **EASY**

This highly ornamental deciduous shrub works terrifically well as a wall climber. It has large, salmon pink flowers with yellow centres borne on bare stems in early spring, followed by fragrant green or yellow fruits. The fruits can be used to make jams and jellies. To train this as a wall climber, set up a framework of wires and tie in the horizontal stems as they develop.

BEST USES A reliable, attractive wall shrub with early spring display, shown to best effect against a wall at the back of a border

FLOWERS March to May

SCENTED Scented fruits

ASPECT Any, in a sheltered or exposed position; full sun to partial shade

SOIL Most moist, fertile, well-drained soils; very limey soil can cause leaf sickness

HARDINESS Fully hardy at temperatures down to -15°C/5°F; needs no winter protection

DROUGHT TOLERANCE Excellent, once established

PROBLEMS Aphids and brown scale; fireblight

PRUNING Prune side shoots after flowering to six leaves and remove any crossed or distorted stems

PROPAGATION Sow seed in autumn; hardwood cuttings September to January; layering in autumn

Chaenomeles speciosa 'Moerloosei' ⚇
Flowering quince

⬆ 2.5m/8ft ⬌ 4m/13ft   **EASY**

A vigorous, deciduous, ornamental shrub that works very well as a wall climber, trained on a framework of wires. It has shiny, dark green leaves and large, white-tinged pink flowers that resemble apple blossom. The flowers are followed by greenish fruits which can be used to make jams and jellies.

BEST USES A lovely wall shrub for early spring interest, probably best grown on a wall at the back of a border but would also suit a courtyard, a wall near a kitchen or cottage garden setting

FLOWERS March to May

SCENTED Fragrant fruits

ASPECT Any, in a sheltered or exposed position; full sun to partial shade

SOIL Most moist, fertile, well-drained soils; very limey soil can cause leaf sickness

HARDINESS Fully hardy at temperatures down to -15°C/5°F; needs no winter protection

DROUGHT TOLERANCE Excellent, once established

PROBLEMS Aphids and brown scale; fireblight

PRUNING Prune side shoots after flowering to six leaves and remove any crossed or distorted stems

PROPAGATION Sow seed in autumn; hardwood cuttings September to January; layering in autumn

Clematis cirrhosa 'Wisley Cream' 🏅

⬆ 4m/13ft ⬌ 90cm/3ft   EASY

A very striking, evergreen tendril climber with small, rounded, mid-green leaves that are tinged bronze in autumn. It has large, attractive, cup-shaped creamy flowers up to 10cm/4in across.

BEST USES Excellent for year-long interest, with its evergreen foliage and larger than average creamy flowers; superb in containers on a warm sunny patio or as a wall climber in a sunny border

FLOWERS April to May
SCENTED No
ASPECT West or south facing, in a sheltered position; full sun
SOIL Any moist, fertile, humus-rich, well-drained soil
HARDINESS Fully hardy at temperatures down to -15°C/5°F; needs no winter protection
DROUGHT TOLERANCE Poor
PROBLEMS Aphids and earwigs; clematis wilt
PRUNING Trim lightly after flowering, removing any damaged stems as you go, to keep the climber looking tidy (Group 1)
PROPAGATION Internodal semi-ripe cuttings in mid to late summer; layering late summer to early autumn

GREENFINGER TIP *Clematis like their heads in the sun and their roots cool and moist, so cover the soil round the base of the plant with broken crocks after planting*

Clematis 'Continuity'

⬆ 3.5m/12ft ⬌ 3m/10ft   EASY

An absolute jewel of a clematis with an impressive profusion of flowers in late spring. It has dark green leaves and large white flowers (about 5cm/2in across), tinged with light pink, from late spring to early summer. It is very vigorous and makes a good-sized plant once established.

BEST USES Will happily scramble over a summer house, garden shed or outbuilding, and ideal for containers (though it will need support when grown in pots)

FLOWERS May to June
SCENTED No
ASPECT Any, in a sheltered or exposed position; full sun to partial shade
SOIL TYPE Any moist, fertile, well-drained soil
HARDINESS Half hardy at temperatures down to 0°C/32°F; will need winter protection in all but the mildest areas
DROUGHT TOLERANCE Poor
PROBLEMS Aphids and earwigs; clematis wilt
PRUNING Remove dead or damaged growth after flowering and trim lightly to restrict the growth if growing in a limited space (Group 1)
PROPAGATION Internodal semi-ripe cuttings in mid to late summer; layering late summer to early autumn

Clematis 'Frances Rivis' ⚇

↑ 2.5m/8ft ⟷ 1.2m/4ft   **EASY**

Who can resist this early-flowering clematis? The small, bell-shaped, blue nodding flowers (definitely the bluest of the alpines) and prominent white stamens are indescribably pretty. The delicate flowers are displayed cheerfully in spring and silky seed heads follow the flowers in late summer to autumn. When I first sighted this little gem, I thought it had been hand-painted by angels.

BEST USES Ideal for training along a small fence or low wall, or for an arbour in the cottage garden; perfect for containers because of its moderate growth habit

FLOWERS April to May
SCENTED No
ASPECT East, south or west facing, in a sheltered or exposed position; full sun to partial shade
SOIL Any moist, fertile, humus-rich, well-drained soil
HARDINESS Fully hardy at temperatures down to -15°C/5°F; needs no winter protection
DROUGHT TOLERANCE Poor
PROBLEMS Aphids and earwigs; clematis wilt
PRUNING Remove dead or damaged growth and trim lightly after flowering to maintain its shape and size (Group 1)
PROPAGATION Internodal semi-ripe cuttings in mid to late summer; layering late summer to early autumn

GREENFINGER TIP *This plant flowers earlier than many other varieties, so is well worth growing for spring interest*

Clematis 'Helsingborg' ⚇

↑ 3m/10ft ⟷ 90cm/3ft   **EASY**

An early-flowering clematis that produces a mass of single, bell-shaped flowers of almost royal purple blue that hang from plum-coloured stems. The leaves are a fresh green and it has very attractive cream stamens. It is both charming and reliable in its flowering display, and excellent for those who are looking for a flowering climber on north-facing walls.

BEST USES Ideal for north- or east-facing walls or trained up partially shaded pillars

FLOWERS April to May
SCENTED No
ASPECT Any, in a sheltered or exposed position; full sun to partial shade
SOIL Any moist, fertile, well-drained soil
HARDINESS Fully hardy at temperatures down to -15°C/5°F; needs no winter protection except in the coldest regions
DROUGHT TOLERANCE Poor
PROBLEMS Aphids and earwigs; clematis wilt
PRUNING Trim lightly after flowering, removing dead or damaged material (Group 1)
PROPAGATION Internodal semi-ripe cuttings in mid to late summer; layering late summer to early autumn

Clematis 'Nelly Moser'

⬆ 2–3m/6–10ft ⬌ 90cm/3ft   EASY

This clematis remains an enduring favourite, so therefore must be mentioned. Perhaps the fact that it excels in shade (though flowering will be reduced) accounts for its popularity. It has mid-green leaves and very large, eye-catching single flowers of pale lilac-pink with carmine striping through the petals.

> **BEST USES** Particularly useful for north-facing walls, and against trellis, pillars and fences

FLOWERS April to June, with a second flush in September

SCENTED No

ASPECT Any, in a sheltered or exposed position; full sun to partial shade

SOIL Any moist, fertile, well-drained soil

HARDINESS Fully hardy at temperatures down to -15°C/5°F; needs no winter protection

DROUGHT TOLERANCE Poor

PROBLEMS Aphids and earwigs; clematis wilt; flowers fade in bright, direct sunlight

PRUNING Remove dead or damaged material in February, before new growth begins; deadhead faded flowers immediately to encourage a second show in late summer or early autumn (Group 2)

PROPAGATION Internodal semi-ripe cuttings in mid to late summer; layering late summer to early autumn

Clematis 'Purple Spider'

⬆ 2.5m/8ft ⬌ 2.5m/8ft   EASY

Here is a knockout spring-flowering clematis that will seduce you from the moment you clap eyes on it. I'm always a pushover for the dark purples, and this ragged, pendent flower is almost black in its richness, highlighted by golden centres, and the sepals curl downward in a spidery display. They flower pretty freely and have beautiful silken seed heads after flowering. What more could you ask?

> **BEST USES** Just gorgeous set against the vivid fresh green foliage of shrubs in spring, and especially handsome with gold-leaved shrubs, such as choisya

FLOWERS April to May

SCENTED No

ASPECT Any, in a sheltered or exposed position; full sun to partial shade

SOIL Any moist, fertile, well-drained soil

HARDINESS Fully hardy at temperatures down to -15°C/5°F; needs no winter protection

DROUGHT TOLERANCE Poor

PROBLEMS Aphids and earwigs; clematis wilt

PRUNING Remove spent or faded flowers and any dead or damaged growth, and trim lightly to restrict height and spread (Group 1)

PROPAGATION Internodal semi-ripe cuttings in mid to late summer; layering late summer to early autumn

Jasminum mesnyi ♀
Primrose jasmine

⬆ 2m/6ft ⬌ 90cm/3ft   EASY

This half-hardy, scrambling evergreen shrub produces a cascade of cheerful, bright yellow single and double flowers in spring. It is a lax shrub (like *J. nudiflorum*), with an elegant, open habit, and will require a sturdy supporting framework when grown as a climber.

BEST USES Perfect for adding an exotic accent to a sunny, warm, sheltered courtyard or terrace; in colder areas, best grown as a conservatory or greenhouse plant and moved outside in summer

FLOWERS March to May
SCENTED No
ASPECT West, south and south-west facing, in a sheltered position with protection from cold winds; full sun to partial shade (flowering is reduced in shade)
SOIL Any moist, fertile, well-drained soil
HARDINESS Half hardy at temperatures down to 0°C/32°F; needs winter protection
DROUGHT TOLERANCE Good, once established
PROBLEMS None outdoors; aphids and mealybug when grown under glass
PRUNING Trim lightly after flowering, removing dead or damaged material to reduce overcrowding
PROPAGATION Softwood or semi-ripe cuttings in spring or summer; hardwood cuttings in winter; layering in spring

GREENFINGER TIP *Remains reliably evergreen if planted at the foot of a sheltered west- or south-facing wall, but will suffer leaf loss in exposed sites*

Rosa 'Danse du Feu'

⬆ 2.5m/8ft ⬌ 30cm/12 inches   EASY

An enduringly popular modern climbing rose with bright, glossy green leaves and upright stems bearing generous clusters of orange-scarlet double flowers exuding a light citrus fragrance. It offers repeat flowering in autumn, though the second display is more modest. The flowers fade to a muted plum as they age, but it is very free-flowering. It is also shade tolerant, so perfect for north walls.

BEST USES Ideal trained up pillars and pergolas and well worth trying on a north-facing wall, though it won't flower as prolifically as in full sun

FLOWERS March to June, and again in September
SCENTED Yes
ASPECT Any, in a sheltered or exposed position; full sun to partial shade
SOIL Any moist, fertile, well-drained soil
HARDINESS Fully hardy at temperatures down to -15°C/5°F; needs no winter protection
DROUGHT TOLERANCE Excellent, once established
PROBLEMS Aphids; blackspot and rust
PRUNING Minimal; cut out damaged stems in late autumn to early spring
PROPAGATION Hardwood cuttings in late autumn

GREENFINGER TIP *This rose is easy to grow and has a repeat flowering habit from summer to autumn, so it isn't a one-season wonder. It also seems to suffer less from disease than other roses*

Clematis 'Apple Blossom' ♛

⬆ 4.5m/15ft ⬌ 3m/10ft   EASY

An indispensable early-flowering clematis with an almondy fragrance (rather like *C. armandii*). It has pretty white flowers, suffused with pale pink. It is a vigorous evergreen tendril climber with attractive mid-green leaves that are slightly bronzed as they unfurl.

BEST USES Plant near doorways or over well-travelled garden arches so the perfume can be appreciated in winter

FLOWERS March to April

SCENTED Fragrant flowers

ASPECT West or south facing, in a sheltered position with protection from cold winds; full sun

SOIL Any moist, fertile, well-drained soil

HARDINESS Frost hardy at temperatures down to -5°C/23°F; may need winter protection in all but the mildest areas

DROUGHT TOLERANCE Poor

PROBLEMS Aphids, caterpillars and earwigs; clematis wilt

PRUNING Remove dead or damaged growth after flowering and trim lightly to restrict the size if growing in a limited space (Group 1)

PROPAGATION Internodal semi-ripe cuttings in mid to late summer; layering late summer to early autumn

GREENFINGER TIP *Feed regularly at monthly intervals during the growing season; if you are short of time, use a slow-release fertiliser*

Clematis armandii

⬆ 8m/26ft ⬌ 4m/13ft   EASY

Originally from China, this vigorous tendril climber has long, leathery, glossy strap-like leaves that are very architectural and look good all year. The stems will need to be tied in to a framework of garden wires as they grow. In spring the exuberant creamy white flowers smell slightly of jasmine. Definitely one of the all-time greats.

BEST USES Site near a doorway or house entrance, where the scent will make you dream of warm days ahead; looks elegant trained along wrought-iron fences or covering outdoor spiral staircases.

FLOWERS March to April

SCENTED Fragrant flowers

ASPECT West or south facing, in a sheltered position with protection from cold winds; full sun

SOIL Any moist, fertile, well-drained soil

HARDINESS Frost hardy at temperatures down to -5°C/23°F; may need winter protection in all but the mildest areas

DROUGHT TOLERANCE Poor

PROBLEMS Aphids, caterpillars and earwigs; clematis wilt

PRUNING Trim back after flowering; if it is getting too unruly you can cut this back fairly hard and new shoots grow away in no time at all (Group 1)

PROPAGATION Internodal semi-ripe cuttings in mid to late summer; layering late summer to early autumn

GREENFINGER TIP *Ensure it is watered regularly during dry weather, or the leaves tend to scorch and brown*

Clematis montana var. *rubens* 'Pink Perfection'

↑ 8m/26ft ↔ 3m/10ft   **EASY**

A vigorous spring-flowering clematis with mid-green leaves, flushed with purple. It bears a profusion of small, sweetly scented, pale rose-coloured flowers in late spring. Reliable, a mad flowerer, easy to look after – and anyway, how could you resist the name?

BEST USES Leave to scramble carelessly over walls, fences, sheds or old outbuildings

FLOWERS May to June

SCENTED Scented flowers

ASPECT Any, in a sheltered or exposed position; full sun to partial shade

SOIL Any moist, fertile, well-drained soil

HARDINESS Fully hardy at temperatures down to -15°C/5°F; needs no winter protection

DROUGHT TOLERANCE Poor

PROBLEMS Aphids, caterpillars and earwigs; clematis wilt

PRUNING Remove dead or damaged growth after flowering, and trim lightly to restrict the growth to size and space (Group 1)

PROPAGATION Internodal semi-ripe cuttings in mid to late summer; layering late summer to early autumn

Clematis montana var. *rubens* 'Tetrarose'

↑ 8m/26ft ↔ 3m/10ft   **EASY**

An understandably popular, vigorous clematis and one of the longer-flowering varieties, with a light, almond scent and deep pink flowers that are larger than some of the other montana varieties. The purplish hues of the young leaves are an attractive feature of this variety, but it's the abundance of flowers that makes this clematis such a worthwhile investment.

BEST USES Marvellously rewarding and dependable for growing over sheds, outbuildings and large runs of fencing; also useful for clothing large trees

FLOWERS May to June

SCENTED Lightly scented flowers

ASPECT Any, in a sheltered or exposed position; full sun to partial shade

SOIL TYPE Any moist, fertile, well-drained soil

HARDINESS Fully hardy at temperatures down to -15°C/5°F; needs no winter protection

DROUGHT TOLERANCE Poor

PROBLEMS Aphids and caterpillars; clematis wilt

PRUNING Trim back after flowering to maintain its allotted size and space (Group 1)

PROPAGATION Internodal semi-ripe cuttings in mid to late summer; layering late summer to early autumn

Holboellia coriacea
Sausage vine

⬆ 8m/26ft ⬌ 4m/13ft   MEDIUM

The sausage vine is a rampant, woody-stemmed evergreen climber with glossy, palm-shaped leaves with a leathery touch. In spring it bears purple male flowers and fat, pale green-white female flowers. The curious fruits borne in autumn are sausage-shaped, hence the common name. They are edible, but not that tasty. Sturdy supports are essential from an early stage as this plant can get weighty.

BEST USES Excellent for growing on trellis or training up garden walls to provide instant spring impact; it always provokes lively interest

FLOWERS March to April

SCENTED No

ASPECT Any, in a sheltered position providing protection from cold winds; full sun to full shade (though it needs sun to produce flowers)

SOIL Any fertile, well-drained soil

HARDINESS Frost hardy at temperatures down to -5°C/23°F; young plants will require protection from frosts

DROUGHT TOLERANCE Poor

PROBLEMS None

PRUNING No regular pruning necessary, trim lightly to restrict it to its allocated space

PROPAGATION Sow seed in spring; semi-ripe cuttings from late summer to autumn; layering in autumn

Lonicera periclymenum 'Belgica'
Early Dutch honeysuckle

⬆ 7m/22ft ⬌ 90cm/3ft   EASY

Grow this vigorous, twining honeysuckle for its gorgeous perfume. It has oval, mid-green leaves and a profusion of sweetly scented tubular flowers, creamy apricot in colour with appealing rosy streaks, which appear earlier than most honeysuckles, in late spring and summer. Red berries follow the flowers in autumn.

BEST USES Very much at home in the cottage, wildlife or woodland garden, where it can be trained into trees and over old stumps or along a rickety fence, and pollinating insects find it very appealing: informal flowering charm at its best

FLOWERS May to June (often into July)

SCENTED Scented flowers

ASPECT Any, in a sheltered or exposed position; full sun to partial shade

SOIL Any moist, fertile, humus-rich, well-drained soil

HARDINESS Fully hardy at temperatures down to -15°C/5°F; needs no winter protection

DROUGHT TOLERANCE Poor

PROBLEMS None

PRUNING Established plants can be cut back to healthy young growth after flowering

PROPAGATION Softwood or semi-ripe cuttings in spring to late summer; hardwood cuttings in late autumn to mid-winter; layering in spring

Akebia quinata
Chocolate vine

⬆ 12m/40ft ⬌ 3m/10ft   **EASY**

This vigorous semi-evergreen to deciduous climber has dapper mid-green, lobed leaves that are attractive in their own right. But it is really grown for its opulent, brooding, chocolate-maroon flowers, which appear in spring and have a light, vanilla-like fragrance. After long hot summers, dark purplish sausage-like fruits are sometimes produced. It needs strong support from the outset as it can get fairly heavy. This is a must-have for those who love sumptuousness and fancy something a bit unusual.

BEST USES Excellent for growing over sturdy trellis or left to scramble through shrubs and small trees

FLOWERS March to April

SCENTED Scented flowers

ASPECT Any, in a sheltered position; full sun to partial shade (though flowering is reduced in shade)

SOIL Any moist, fertile, well-drained soil

HARDINESS Fully hardy; mature plants withstand temperatures down to -20°C/-4°F, but young plants need protection from cold and frosts

DROUGHT TOLERANCE Poor

PROBLEMS None; plant in the right spot first time, as it resents root disturbance

PRUNING Trim lightly after flowering

PROPAGATION Sow cold stratified seed in spring; greenwood cuttings from late spring to mid-summer; layering in autumn and early spring

Akebia trifoliata
Three-leaved akebia

⬆ 12m/40ft ⬌ 8m/26ft   **EASY**

Here's a slightly unusual climber, semi-evergreen in all but the coldest areas, which has oval, lightly serrated leaves that have a pale purple tint when young, darkening to glossy green as the plant matures. Its flowers, although unscented, are pendent, shallowly cupped and a beautiful chocolate purple colour, followed by purple sausage-shaped fruits in autumn.

BEST USES Perfect for walls and trellis, adding a touch of late-spring interest; the flowers and leaves are well worth combining with a summer-flowering climber (possibly one of the large clematis hybrids?)

FLOWERS April to May

SCENTED No

ASPECT Any, in a sheltered or exposed position; full sun to partial shade

SOIL Any moist, fertile, well-drained soil

HARDINESS Fully hardy at temperatures down to -15°C/5°F; needs no winter protection

DROUGHT TOLERANCE Poor

PROBLEMS None; plant in the right spot first time, as it resents root disturbance

PRUNING Prune regularly and lightly after flowering to restrict size and shape

PROPAGATION Sow cold stratified seed in spring; greenwood cuttings from late spring to mid-summer; layering in autumn and early spring

GREENFINGER TIP *This can get quite invasive once it settles down, so keep a watchful eye on its expansion!*

Clematis 'Elizabeth'

12m/40ft ↔ 4m/13ft EASY

A vigorous deciduous tendrilled climber that is easy to grow. It has attractive dark green tri-lobed leaves and simply masses of pale pink, lightly scented flowers in late spring to early summer.

BEST USES Perfect for large walls, pergolas and trellis and for covering unsightly outbuildings

FLOWERS May to June
SCENTED Scented flowers
ASPECT Any, in a sheltered or exposed position; full sun to partial shade (though flowering may be reduced in shade)
SOIL Any moist, fertile, well-drained soil
HARDINESS Fully hardy at temperatures down to -15°C/5°F; needs no winter protection
DROUGHT TOLERANCE Poor
PROBLEMS Aphids, caterpillars and earwigs; clematis wilt
PRUNING Trim lightly after flowering to restrict size and shape (Group 1)
PROPAGATION Internodal semi-ripe cuttings in mid to late summer; layering late summer to early autumn

Clematis montana var. *grandiflora*

10m/32ft ↔ 4m/13ft EASY

A vigorous deciduous climber that is so easy to grow it's a sure-fire winner. It has dark green lobed leaves and masses of bright, white flowers in late spring to early summer. A reliable and prolific flowering performer.

BEST USES Perfect for walls, pergolas, trellis and outbuildings, and ideal for growing up a large tree

FLOWERS May to June
SCENTED No
ASPECT Any, in a sheltered or exposed position; full sun to partial shade (though flowering is reduced in shade)
SOIL Any moist, fertile, well-drained soil
HARDINESS Fully hardy at temperatures down to -15°C/5°F; needs no winter protection
DROUGHT TOLERANCE Poor
PROBLEMS Aphids, caterpillars and earwigs; clematis wilt
PRUNING Trim lightly after flowering to restrict size and shape (Group 1)
PROPAGATION Internodal semi-ripe cuttings in mid to late summer; layering late summer to early autumn

GREENFINGER TIP *Like all clematis, plant deeply to minimise the risk of clematis wilt*

Clematis montana var. *rubens* 'Odorata'

⬆ 10m/32ft ↔ 4m/13ft   EASY

A reliable, fast-growing, vigorous clematis with mid-green leaves, producing a cascade of pale pink flowers with deeper pink veining from late spring to early summer. The flowers have a light vanilla fragrance and attractive yellow anthers.

BEST USES Will ramble freely over a large wall, shed or unsightly outbuilding, and also ideal for training up a large tree or pergola or over a garden walkway

FLOWERS April to May

SCENTED Lightly scented flowers

ASPECT Any, in a sheltered or exposed position; full sun to partial shade (though flowering is reduced in shade)

SOIL Any moist, fertile, well-drained soil

HARDINESS Fully hardy at temperatures down to -15°C/5°F; needs no winter protection

DROUGHT TOLERANCE Poor

PROBLEMS Aphids and caterpillars; clematis wilt

PRUNING Remove dead or damaged growth after flowering and trim lightly to restrict it to its allocated space (Group 1)

PROPAGATION Internodal semi-ripe cuttings in mid to late summer; layering late summer to early autumn

GREENFINGER TIP *A good mulch of well-rotted manure in spring will keep this climber looking at its best*

Hydrangea anomala subsp. *petiolaris* ♀
Climbing hydrangea

⬆ 15m/50ft ↔ 3m/10ft   EASY

An energetic, woody-stemmed, deciduous climbing hydrangea that is self-clinging and has masses of attractive, lacy white flower heads from late spring to summer. It has large mid-green leaves with serrated edges and is neat in appearance: all in all, a well-behaved, no-nonsense sort of plant.

BEST USES Invaluable for filling large spaces, and excellent for shady city gardens with damp corners where not much else will both thrive and also provide attractive leaf and flower colour; very reliable on north-facing walls

FLOWERS May to July

SCENTED No

ASPECT Any, in a sheltered or exposed position; full sun to partial shade

SOIL Any fertile, well-drained soil

HARDINESS Fully hardy at temperatures down to -15°C/5°F; needs no winter protection

DROUGHT TOLERANCE Good, once established

PROBLEMS None

PRUNING Minimal; cut out unwanted stems and side shoots in late winter or early spring

PROPAGATION Sow seed in spring; softwood cuttings from late spring to mid-summer; semi-ripe cuttings in summer; layering in spring

Lonicera japonica 'Halliana' ♊
Japanese honeysuckle 'Halliana', Hall's honeysuckle

⬆ 10m/32ft ↔ 3m/10ft   EASY

This vigorous evergreen honeysuckle from Japan is smothered in highly scented, pure white tubular flowers, which are smaller than other honeysuckles, from spring to late summer. As the flowers mature they age to dark yellow. The leaves are dark green, and shiny black berries are produced in autumn. Attractive to wildlife and a really worthwhile investment for its long flowering period and evergreen nature.

BEST USES Will scramble happily over outhouses, sheds and garages, looks great combined with clematis or roses, and is particularly useful for coastal gardens as it is tolerant of salt-laden winds

FLOWERS April to August
SCENTED Scented flowers
ASPECT Any, in a sheltered or exposed position; full sun to partial shade
SOIL Any fertile, humus-rich, moist, well-drained soil
HARDINESS Fully hardy at temperatures down to -15°C/5°F; needs no winter protection
DROUGHT TOLERANCE Good, once established
PROBLEMS Powdery mildew
PRUNING After flowering, remove any overcrowded or crossed shoots
PROPAGATION Softwood or semi-ripe cuttings in spring to late summer; hardwood cuttings in late autumn to mid-winter; layering in spring

Rosa banksiae 'Lutea' ♊
Yellow banksian rose

⬆ 9m/30ft ↔ 9m/30ft   EASY

A vigorous early-flowering climbing rose which is also evergreen – although in the mildest areas only – and (almost) thornless. Small, lightly fragrant clusters of pale primrose yellow flowers burst forth in fair abundance from late spring to early summer and are followed by shapely rose hips.

BEST USES Train along a sheltered fence or a large sheltered wall; it combines incredibly well with wisteria as they both flower around the same time

FLOWERS April/May to June
SCENTED Lightly scented flowers
ASPECT East, south and west facing, in a sheltered position with protection from cold winds; full sun
SOIL Any moist, fertile, humus-rich, well-drained soil
HARDINESS Frost hardy at temperatures down to -5°C/23°F; may need winter protection in cold areas
DROUGHT TOLERANCE Good, once established
PROBLEMS Aphids and caterpillars; blackspot, rust and powdery mildew; rabbits
PRUNING None initially, and may be difficult on a mature plant because of its size; deadhead after flowering, and remove dead or damaged wood in late autumn and early spring; every three years, cut back three of the main stems to 45cm/18in above the ground
PROPAGATION Hardwood cuttings in late autumn

....
GREENFINGER TIP *This can be slow to establish, but it will soon spread, so make sure you give it plenty of space*

Schisandra rubriflora

⬆ 10m/32ft ↔ 6m/20ft   **EASY**

I love this elegant deciduous climber. It is actually related to the magnolias, though the connection isn't an obvious one, for it is a woody climber of medium size, with vigorously twining stems and small deep green leaves with lightly serrated edges. In summer, it bears striking, pendulous clusters of scented, scarlet cup-shaped flowers. After flowering, hanging bunches of vivid red berries are borne on the female plants. It offers enormous year-round interest.

BEST USES The stunning summer flowers are especially useful for a hot colour flower border; the autumn berries are a good lure for birds

FLOWERS May to June
SCENTED Scented flowers
ASPECT East, south or west facing, in a sheltered position with protection from cold winds; full sun to partial shade
SOIL Any moist, humus-rich, well-drained soil
HARDINESS Fully hardy at temperatures down to -15°C/5°F; needs no winter protection
DROUGHT TOLERANCE Poor
PROBLEMS None
PRUNING Minimal; cut back or remove unwanted branches in spring, and tie in young shoots to establish a framework in the first two seasons
PROPAGATION Layering in autumn or winter

Stauntonia hexaphylla

⬆ 9m/30ft ↔ 2.5m/8ft   **MEDIUM**

This fast-growing evergreen climber has rather handsome, dark green, leathery leaves and very pretty, cupped, pendent, fragrant flowers, white stained violet. After long hot summers, small purple fruits may be produced.

BEST USES Site on a warm south- or west-facing wall with shading from direct sunlight; grow as an annual in colder regions or overwinter in a frost-free greenhouse and move to a sheltered sunny spot in summer

FLOWERS April to May
SCENTED Scented flowers
ASPECT South or west facing, in a sheltered position; full sun to partial shade
SOIL Any moist, fertile, well-drained soil
HARDINESS Frost hardy at temperatures down to -5°C/23°F; may need winter protection
DROUGHT TOLERANCE Poor
PROBLEMS None
PRUNING Remove dead or damaged growth after flowering and trim lightly to restrict the plant to its allocated space
PROPAGATION Sow seed in spring at 13–16°C/55–61°F; semi-ripe cuttings in summer

GREENFINGER TIP *In the growing season, water freely and apply a balanced proprietary plant feed once a month, but keep it drier in the winter months*

Wisteria

Wisteria sinensis 'Alba'

isteria is the king of climbers. It is the most stately of climbing plants, with an imperial elegance, enchanting fragrance and the most spectacular flowers.

The wisterias are vigorous twining deciduous climbers with light green pinnate leaves, but it is the fragrant chandeliered flowers that make them so admired. There are a great many varieties to choose from, some with larger flower pendants than others, and each with its own individual appeal. All, without exception, are highly perfumed, widely esteemed and ornamental.

As this is such a potentially large climber, take time to plant it in an ideal spot, where it has plenty of room to grow. Some are tempted to grow wisteria over a large garden structure but, because of the relatively brief flowering period, it is best teamed up with later-flowering clematis or roses to extend the period of interest.

Whichever wisteria you plump for, they all need:

- full sun
- fertile, well-drained soil
- strong supports from the outset – wisterias are potentially very large, heavy plants in maturity, and a few spindly garden wires are not going to do the job adequately
- careful formative pruning, to prevent them being all leaf and no flower

A lot of kerfuffle is made of pruning wisteria and I am sure this puts a great many people off growing it, but the pruning is not nearly as tricky as some like to make out. It is potentially a very large climber, so some control to restrict its eventual height and size is a consideration especially when it is grown on the wall of a house, to avoid damage to roof tiles and gutters.

Alternatively, wisteria can be trained as a standard tree or, if you have a large space, you can let it grow freely without any interference at all. I have a lovely specimen growing through a mature *Magnolia grandiflora* and the two manage to complement each other beautifully, without any major intervention on my part.

However, if you want to train it as a climber in a restricted space, pruning twice a year, in summer and winter, improves the flowering tremendously and keeps it manageable.

August pruning

After flowering has finished, look for gaps in the developing framework. Tie in appropriate stems to fill any gaps in the display. Cut back the rest of the current season's shoots to approximately 30cm/12in from the point from which they have grown. This allows space for the sun to get in to ripen the wood, encouraging young shoots and flower buds to form.

Numerous side shoots will appear throughout the growing season, both from the main stems and from the horizontal shoots that grow from these. The side shoots will go on to form future flower buds, but 'shortening' or pruning them encourages flowering spurs. The more shortening you carry out, the more flowers you will develop. Long whippy shoots will develop after the summer pruning – ignore them, as these will be cut back in winter.

Removing excess or unwanted shoots effectively prevents the plant putting all its energy into keeping copious stems growing. This allows it to divert its energy into forming a more limited amount of flower buds which will be fatter and more spectacular once they flower.

February pruning

Cut back the side shoots that were pruned in the summer to two or three buds or within 3–5cm/1–2in of the old wood (which is darker in colour than the new wood, and woody in texture). Angle each cut so that rainwater drains off the stem away from the developing bud. Short, stubby shoots or spurs will be left, and the fatter, potential flower buds will be easy to distinguish from the slimmer growth buds, which will make new shoots.

The long, whippy shoots that grew after the previous August's pruning can also be cut back to five or six buds from the main branch, making the cut just after a bud. As you prune, be very careful not to knock the fat flower buds, which damage easily: these are where the flowers will develop.

February is also an ideal time to cut back or remove old woody branches that are getting out of control or growing away from their supports or walls. At the same time, mulch with organic matter at the base to encourage healthy growth.

A word to the wise is needed here: always buy a grafted wisteria from a reputable grower and buy it in flower: there are some unsavoury growers out there who will flog you a wisteria that has been grown from seed and may take seven or more years to flower or, worse still, not flower at all.

The king of climbers, wisteria is also incredibly drought resistant

Wisteria floribunda 'Multijuga' ☙
(formerly 'Macrobotrys')

⬆ 9m/30ft ⬌ 9m/30ft — **EASY**

This variety of wisteria has pale green leaves and highly scented pendants of pale violet flowers which are longer than average and produced from late spring to summer. They are followed by velvety seed pods.

> **BEST USES** Perfect for gracing either the front or rear of a large house wall; alternatively, let it grow freely through a large tree

FLOWERS May to June
SCENTED Very fragrant flowers
ASPECT South or west facing, in a sheltered position; full sun, though flowers reasonably well in partial shade
SOIL Any moist, fertile, well-drained soil
HARDINESS Fully hardy at temperatures down to -15°C/5°F; needs no winter protection
DROUGHT TOLERANCE Excellent, once established
PROBLEMS Frosts may sometimes damage flower buds, particularly if planted on east-facing walls
PRUNING See pages 24–5
PROPAGATION Sow seed in early spring; softwood cuttings in spring to mid-summer; hardwood cuttings in winter; layering in winter

GREENFINGER TIP *A nurseryman of my acquaintance has this growing in 6m/20ft depth of sandy soil and it continues to flourish without extra watering or feeding. If you have similar soil, give it a go: wisteria is incredibly drought tolerant*

Wisteria floribunda 'Rosea' ☙
Pink Japanese wisteria

⬆ 9m/30ft ⬌ 4m/13ft — **EASY**

This is slightly less vigorous than Chinese wisteria (*W. sinensis*), though it achieves a good size, and curiously twines from right to left, whereas Chinese wisteria twines in an anti-clockwise direction. Pink Japanese wisteria has pale pink flowers hanging down in spectacular perfumed clusters, followed by velvety green-grey seed pods.

> **BEST USES** Ideal for growing over a large sturdy pergola or gazebo, or trained to cover a long length of fencing or a west-facing wall

FLOWERS May to June
SCENTED Highly scented flowers
ASPECT South or west facing, in a sheltered position; full sun, though flowers reasonably well in partial shade
SOIL Any moist, fertile, well-drained soil
HARDINESS Fully hardy at temperatures down to -15°C/5°F; needs no winter protection
DROUGHT TOLERANCE Excellent, once established
PROBLEMS Frosts may sometimes damage flower buds, particularly if planted on east-facing walls
PRUNING See pages 24–5
PROPAGATION Sow seed in early spring; softwood cuttings in spring to mid-summer; hardwood cuttings in winter; layering in winter

Wisteria sinensis 🏅
Chinese wisteria

⬆ 15m/50ft ⬌ 12m/40ft   EASY

Wisteria sinensis has long, pendulous, sweetly perfumed, pale lilac-blue flowers which are produced in abundance in late spring and early summer – rather resembling a splendid tiered chandelier. The flowers are produced on bare stems, with the leaves appearing as the flowers fade. After flowering, long velvety pea pods are formed.

BEST USES Ideal left to scramble freely through a large tree to enhance spring interest, or can be trained as a standard tree; combines beautifully with the yellow *Rosa banksiae* 'Lutea' (see page 22)

FLOWERS May to June
SCENTED Scented flowers
ASPECT South or west facing, in a sheltered position; full sun, though flowers reasonably well in partial shade
SOIL Any moist, fertile, well-drained soil
HARDINESS Fully hardy at temperatures down to -15°C/5°F; needs no winter protection
DROUGHT TOLERANCE Excellent, once established
PROBLEMS Frosts may sometimes damage flower buds, particularly if planted on east-facing walls
PRUNING See pages 24–5
PROPAGATION Sow seed in early spring; softwood cuttings in spring to mid-summer; hardwood cuttings in winter; layering in winter

Wisteria sinensis 'Alba' 🏅
White Chinese wisteria

⬆ 9m/30ft ⬌ 5m/16ft   EASY

Wisteria sinensis 'Alba' has sumptuous pendent tassels of highly perfumed, pure white flowers up to 60cm/24in long in late spring and early summer. The flowers are produced on bare stems, with the leaves appearing as the flowers fade. After flowering, pale green-grey velvety pea pods are formed. It is less vigorous in its growth than other varieties.

BEST USES Ideal for growing along a sunny wall or training across the front of the house

FLOWERS June
SCENTED Scented flowers
ASPECT South or west facing, in a sheltered position; full sun, though flowers reasonably well in partial shade
SOIL Any moist, fertile, well-drained soil
HARDINESS Fully hardy at temperatures down to -15°C/5°F; needs no winter protection
DROUGHT TOLERANCE Excellent, once established
PROBLEMS Frosts may sometimes damage flower buds, particularly if planted on east-facing walls
PRUNING See pages 24–5
PROPAGATION Sow seed in early spring; softwood cuttings in spring to mid-summer; hardwood cuttings in winter; layering in winter

SUMMER

'Summer afternoons — summer afternoons ... the two most beautiful words in the English language.'

HENRY JAMES

Most gardeners love the summer garden. Everything is in full flower, colour bursts forth from the borders, rose scents perfume the air, butterflies whirl, bees drone, the sun is high in the sky, warming our cheeks, and all those tireless months of garden labour are rewarding you now. Clothe your garden walls, fences and small trees in summer-flowering climbers and you will find they add a sense of floral sanctuary to the existing garden tapestry.

Abutilon megapotamicum ♻
Trailing abutilon

⬆ 2m/6ft ⬌ 2m/6ft   **MEDIUM**

This tender, deciduous to evergreen shrub from Brazil is often described as an arching shrub, though in reality it is more lax in its growth habit. It has bright yellow and red pendent flowers that resemble rather curious exotic hanging lanterns from spring through to autumn.

BEST USES Great for conservatories or greenhouses, though it can be grown outside in containers or as a border plant on a sunny, sheltered patio in very mild areas

FLOWERS April to September
SCENTED No
ASPECT East or south facing, in a sheltered position; full sun to partial shade (it enjoys sun in the morning with light shade on hot afternoons)
SOIL Any fertile, well-drained soil, preferably loam or sand
HARDINESS Half hardy at temperatures down to 0°C/32°F; needs winter protection or overwinter in a frost-free greenhouse in colder areas
DROUGHT TOLERANCE Good, once established
PROBLEMS Aphids, mealybug and whitefly
PRUNING Minimal; prune lightly by removing unsightly or frost-damaged shoots from mid-spring
PROPAGATION Sow seed in spring at 15–18°C/ 59–64°F; softwood, greenwood or semi-ripe cuttings at any time; hardwood cuttings in autumn

GREENFINGER TIP *This plant can easily become pot-bound, which will cause it to lose its lower leaves and look a bit sad, so re-pot it every two to three years*

Asteranthera ovata

⬆ 4m/13ft ⬌ 2m/6ft   **TRICKY**

This elegant, evergreen creeping climber from South America is high maintenance, only flourishing in exacting conditions, but the small, attractive, deep green shiny leaves and beautiful, deep rose-red, star-shaped tubular flowers throughout the summer are just reward.

BEST USES Useful for containers or as a back of border plant in a sheltered spot; it looks very pretty scrambling across a rockery

FLOWERS June to August

SCENTED No

ASPECT North or west facing, in a sheltered position; partial shade; requires cool, humid conditions

SOIL Any moist, humus-rich, acid soil

HARDINESS Frost hardy at temperatures down to -5°C/23°F; needs winter protection

DROUGHT TOLERANCE Poor

PROBLEMS Aphids

PRUNING Minimal; remove dead or damaged shoots in early spring

PROPAGATION Sow seed on compost surface in autumn; softwood cuttings with bottom heat in spring

....

GREENFINGER TIP *If you're up for a challenge this is a super plant. You will need to establish a good feeding and watering regime (providing a monthly liquid feed, and watering freely in the growing season) AND offer exactly the right conditions of humidity (plant it near a watered area, cascade or garden waterfall, out of direct sunlight). I wish you luck!*

Berberidopsis corallina
Coral plant

⬆ 3–3.5m/10–12ft ⬌ 2m/6ft   **TRICKY**

This is a real stunner, known as the coral plant because of the flamboyant red tubular flowers which hang from the stems rather like bunches of berries. They appear from summer to early autumn and are displayed attractively in pendent clusters against the more upright, bright green, toothed oval leaves.

BEST USES An unusual, exotic climber for sheltered sites to bring a touch of colourful glamour to the garden

FLOWERS July to September

SCENTED No

ASPECT East or west facing, in a sheltered position; partial shade

SOIL Moist, humus-rich, well-drained acid soil; will tolerate slightly chalky soil; add organic matter

HARDINESS Frost hardy at temperatures down to -5°C/23°F; protect the roots with a mulch or fleece in winter

DROUGHT TOLERANCE Poor

PROBLEMS Will not tolerate cold winds

PRUNING Minimal; prune out the dead and overcrowded growth in late winter/early spring

PROPAGATION Sow seed in spring; semi-ripe cuttings in late summer; layering in autumn

....

GREENFINGER TIP *In my experience, this is unbelievably sensitive to cold winds, but if you can provide a sheltered site in moist shade, similar to its woodland origins, it should thrive happily. Well worth a shot, as it's a real stunner*

Bougainvillea x *buttiana* 'Mrs Butt' ☿
Paper flower

⬆ 3m/10ft ⬌ 4m/13ft   **TRICKY**

Bougainvillea is a woody-stemmed, branching thorny climber with vivid cerise pink papery flower bracts and is deciduous in cold regions. Although I have seen it grown successfully in a Cornish garden, elsewhere I would only grow it as an indoor plant. It is best tied in to a strong supporting framework. Grown outdoors in hot climates, it can attain a height of 10m/32ft.

BEST USES Grow as a conservatory plant in a large planter as it is not suitable for a small pot

FLOWERS July to September
SCENTED No
ASPECT South or west facing, in an enclosed sheltered position in very mild areas; full sun
SOIL Any fertile, well-drained soil, preferably loam or sand
HARDINESS Half hardy at temperatures down to 0°C/32°F; best kept above 7°C/45°F or it goes into dormancy and loses all its leaves; keep touch-dry in winter
DROUGHT TOLERANCE Good, once established
PROBLEMS Red spider mite when grown indoors; dislikes fluctuating temperatures
PRUNING Trim lightly after flowering to maintain shape and spread and encourage new growth; cut side shoots back to 2–3 buds in February once actively growing
PROPAGATION Heeled softwood cuttings in spring or semi-ripe cuttings with bottom heat in summer; layering in early spring or late winter

Calystegia hederacea 'Flore Pleno'
Bind plant

⬆ 3.5m/12ft ⬌ 90cm/3ft   **EASY**

This rare, tender, vigorous twining climber is worth growing for the profusion of shell pink flowers produced in the summer months. It is very easy to cultivate, so perhaps the fact it can be invasive puts people off. In colder areas it is best grown as an annual.

BEST USES Can be extremely invasive, so best grown in a container or patio pot (it will need frequent re-potting as it grows so quickly), or as a summer annual trained up garden trellis or at the foot of a warm south-facing wall; also ideal for sheltered coastal gardens

FLOWERS June to August
SCENTED No
ASPECT South or west facing, in a sheltered or exposed position; full sun
SOIL Most moist, fertile, well-drained soils; struggles in heavy clay
HARDINESS Frost tender, not hardy at temperatures below 5°C/41°F; grow in a frost-free greenhouse and move to a warm sunny position outside in summer
DROUGHT TOLERANCE Poor
PROBLEMS Aphids
PRUNING None; will die back naturally with the first frosts
PROPAGATION Sow seed in spring

GREENFINGER TIP *The sunnier the position the more profuse the flowering*

Clematis x durandii 🎖

⬆ 1.5m/5ft ↔ 90cm/3ft   **EASY**

A delightful herbaceous clematis of low scrambling habit that has medium-sized indigo flowers and contrasting white stamens. A charming and very eye-catching climber that is easy to manage.

BEST USES Leave to lace its way through low-growing perennials; makes a striking contrast against orange- or yellow-flowering plants

FLOWERS June to September

SCENTED No

ASPECT Any, in a sheltered or exposed position; full sun to partial shade

SOIL Any humus-rich, moist, fertile, well-drained soil

HARDINESS Frost hardy at temperatures down to -5°C/23°F; protect with a mulch or fleece in winter

DROUGHT TOLERANCE Poor

PROBLEMS Earwigs; clematis wilt

PRUNING In mid-February, before the emergence of new growth, cut back to about 15cm/6in above ground level, leaving a good pair of strong buds (Group 3)

PROPAGATION Division in autumn or early spring

• •

GREENFINGER TIP *This may benefit from staking as it tends to straggle sideways; alternatively, plant it next to sturdy-stemmed plants that will support it in an upright fashion (see pages 92–8)*

Clematis 'Gipsy Queen' 🎖

⬆ 4m/13ft ↔ 4m/13ft   **EASY**

One of my favourite clematis, 'Gipsy Queen' has velvety flowers of deepest purple, making a marked contrast against pretty, lettuce-green leaves. It is very easy to care for, reasonably free flowering, and a must-have for its reliably long flowering period.

BEST USES A beautiful companion grown through climbing roses and honeysuckles, and also does well in a container

FLOWERS July to September

SCENTED No

ASPECT Any, in a sheltered or exposed position; full sun or partial shade

SOIL Any moist, fertile, well-drained soil

HARDINESS Fully hardy at temperatures down to -15°C/5°F; needs no winter protection

DROUGHT TOLERANCE Poor

PROBLEMS Aphids, caterpillars, earwigs and woolly aphids; clematis wilt

PRUNING In early spring, before the emergence of new growth, cut back all the previous year's stems to healthy pairs of buds about 15cm/6in above ground level (Group 3)

PROPAGATION Internodal semi-ripe cuttings in mid to late summer; layering late summer to early autumn

Clematis 'M. Koster'
(formerly 'Margot Koster')

↑ 3.5m/12ft ↔ 4m/13ft   **EASY**

This uncomplicated, reliable clematis is highly recommended for the beginner – satisfaction guaranteed! It is very free flowering, and the large, satin pink flowers have pronounced paler veining down the centres of the petals. It has fresh, mid-green deciduous leaves, and is fairly vigorous. If you cut it back after flowering, it often very obligingly throws out a further, though more modest, crop of flowers.

> **BEST USES** Gorgeous scrambling over shrubs that are long past their flowering best and never smothers its host

FLOWERS July to September
SCENTED No
ASPECT Any, in a sheltered or exposed position; full sun to partial shade
SOIL TYPE Any moist, fertile, well-drained soil
HARDINESS Fully hardy at temperatures down to -15°C/5°F; needs no winter protection
DROUGHT TOLERANCE Poor
PROBLEMS Aphids, caterpillars, earwigs and woolly aphids; clematis wilt
PRUNING In early spring, cut back all the previous year's stems to healthy pairs of buds about 15cm/6in above ground level (Group 3)
PROPAGATION Internodal semi-ripe cuttings in mid to late summer; layering late summer to early autumn

Clematis 'Rosea' ♡

↑ 60cm/2ft ↔ 60cm/2ft   **EASY**

A delightful, scented, herbaceous clematis of low scrambling habit that is easy to care for and has nodding, rose-pink, recurved bell-shaped flowers held high on upright slender stems from summer to early autumn.

> **BEST USES** An ideal companion for enhancing flower borders at low levels, scrambling through other herbaceous plants, or equally stylish weaving through low grasses

FLOWERS July to September
SCENTED Scented flowers
ASPECT Any, in a sheltered or exposed position; full sun to partial shade
SOIL Any humus-rich, moist, fertile, well-drained soil
HARDINESS Frost hardy at temperatures down to -5°C/23°F; protect with a mulch or fleece in winter
DROUGHT TOLERANCE Poor
PROBLEMS Earwigs; clematis wilt
PRUNING In mid-February, cut back to about 15cm/6in above ground level, leaving a good pair of strong buds (Group 3)
PROPAGATION Internodal semi-ripe cuttings in mid to late summer; layering late summer to early autumn

Clematis 'Venosa Violacea' ♟

⬆ 3m/10ft ↔ 4m/13ft　　　　**EASY**

A beautiful deciduous clematis that is fairly fast-growing and bears medium-sized purple flowers with attractive white veining. The leaves are neat and mid-green and it is a robust, reliable grower, taking all weathers except very heavy drought enormously well.

BEST USES A striking clematis that contrasts incredibly well with any golden-foliaged small tree or shrub: gold, yellow and purple always work well together

FLOWERS July to September

SCENTED No

ASPECT Any, in a sheltered or exposed position; full sun to partial shade

SOIL Any moist, fertile, well-drained soil; will thrive in chalky, drier soils

HARDINESS Fully hardy at temperatures down to -15°C/5°F; needs no winter protection

DROUGHT TOLERANCE Poor

PROBLEMS Aphids, caterpillars and earwigs; clematis wilt

PRUNING In early spring, before the emergence of new growth, cut stems back to healthy pairs of buds about 15cm/6in above ground level (Group 3)

PROPAGATION Internodal semi-ripe cuttings in mid to late summer; layering late summer to early autumn

Clianthus puniceus ♟
Lobster claw/Parrot's bill

⬆ 4m/13ft ↔ 4m/13ft　　　　**MEDIUM**

A tender evergreen or semi-evergreen woody climber that has a scrambling habit with dark green strap-like leaves and deep red flowers shaped like a parrot's bill in summer, hence the common name. It may be grown outside in very mild areas only and will need support from the early stages of planting. It also takes to being fan-trained on a sheltered wall.

BEST USES An exotic climber for sun-drenched patio pots in milder areas, but best grown as a greenhouse or conservatory plant in colder regions

FLOWERS June to August

SCENTED No

ASPECT South or west facing, in a sheltered position; full sun

SOIL Any moist, fertile, well-drained soil, particularly loam and sand

HARDINESS Frost hardy at temperatures down to -5°C/23°F; protect the roots with a mulch or fleece in winter, or bring indoors in colder areas

DROUGHT TOLERANCE Poor

PROBLEMS Mealybug and red spider mite when grown in a greenhouse

PRUNING Minimal; trim after flowering to maintain size and shape

PROPAGATION Sow seed in spring at 13–18°C/55–64°F; semi-ripe cuttings in early summer

Eccremocarpus scaber
Chilean glory flower

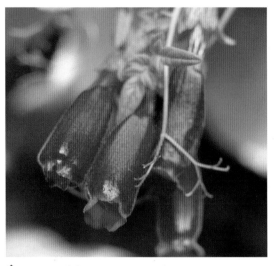

⬆ 3m/10ft ↔ 1.8m/5¾ft **MEDIUM**

The Chilean glory flower is a slender, fast-growing, evergreen perennial climber that is easy to grow, clinging by tendrils, and has ferny, light green leaves. The profusion of tubular orange to red flower clusters which appear from summer to autumn are the winning feature of this climber. Self-sown seedlings will spring up in abundance.

BEST USES Ideal for containers in sunny courtyard gardens or for adding a tropical accent to the garden when trained up trellis

FLOWERS May to November
SCENTED No
ASPECT West or south facing, in a sheltered position protected from cold winds; full sun
SOIL Most well-drained soils, particularly loam and sand; will struggle on heavy clay
HARDINESS Half hardy at temperatures down to 0°C/32°F; protect in winter or grow as an annual
DROUGHT TOLERANCE Good, once established
PROBLEMS Aphids
PRUNING In its first year, cut down to 15cm/6in in spring to encourage new basal growth; in following years, prune back all growth to 60cm/2ft and remove damaged or dead stems
PROPAGATION Sow seed in late winter or early spring at 13–16°C/55–61°F; root tip cuttings with bottom heat in spring or summer

Ipomoea tricolor 'Heavenly Blue' ♀
Morning glory

⬆ 4m/13ft ↔ 90cm/3ft **EASY**

A twining annual climber bearing very attractive, large, bright blue funnelled flowers with contrasting white throats profusely in summer. The flowers are short-lived, but are quickly replaced by new blooms. It's really an ornamental, non-invasive, well-behaved bindweed in disguise!

BEST USES Ideal in containers, or scrambling through herbaceous borders, over shrubs and up small trees

FLOWERS June to October
SCENTED No
ASPECT South or west facing, in a sheltered position; full sun
SOIL Any fertile, well-drained soil
HARDINESS Half hardy at temperatures down to 0°C/32°F; needs greenhouse protection before planting out as an annual in cold areas
DROUGHT TOLERANCE Poor
PROBLEMS None outdoors; red spider mite when grown under glass
PRUNING None; will die back naturally with the first frosts
PROPAGATION Sow seed in spring or early summer at 18°C/64°F

GREENFINGER TIP *Always soak the seed in warm water, to hasten germination, before sowing into compost*

Jasminum beesianum
Red jasmine

⬆ 4m/13ft ↔ 3m/10ft   **EASY**

An unusual, fast-growing, slender deciduous climber that has a charming scrambling habit. It has faintly scented, pinky red velvet tubular flowers during the summer and shiny black berries that last well into winter. The leaves are dark green and lance shaped. It requires firm support from the early planting stages.

BEST USES An ideal container plant for a back door where the fragrant flowers can be fully appreciated; will soon scramble up a hedge or wire framework and blends well with other shrubs, especially dark-coloured flowering shrubs such as *Buddleja davidii* 'Black Knight'

FLOWERS June to July
SCENTED Lightly scented flowers
ASPECT South facing, in a sheltered position; full sun
SOIL Any fertile, well-drained soil
HARDINESS Frost hardy at temperatures down to -5°C/23°F; protect with a mulch or fleece in winter
DROUGHT TOLERANCE Good, once established in the ground; will need regular watering in containers
PROBLEMS Young plants can be prone to frost damage
PRUNING Cut out crossing stems and old shoots directly after flowering
PROPAGATION Softwood or semi-ripe cuttings in spring or summer; hardwood cuttings in winter; layering in spring

••

GREENFINGER TIP *The perfume is stronger when the plant is grown in full sun*

Jasminum officinale 'Clotted Cream'

⬆ 3m/10ft ↔ 3m/10ft   **EASY**

This pretty little climber is a form of *Jasminum officinale*, which has the added benefit of being semi-evergreen in mild areas. In summer it is smothered in masses of sweetly fragrant creamy flowers and is as seductive and dainty as any climber could possibly be.

BEST USES Display against a low wall, fence or climbing up a pergola; also a lovely plant for rooftop gardens, as long as some shelter from winds is provided

FLOWERS July to September
SCENTED Yes
ASPECT South or south-west facing, in a sheltered position; full sun to partial shade
SOIL Any fertile, well-drained soil
HARDINESS Frost hardy at temperatures down to -5°C/23°F; may need winter protection in colder areas
DROUGHT TOLERANCE Excellent, once established
PROBLEMS None
PRUNING Cut out overcrowded or crossed shoots after flowering, and any dead or damaged material
PROPAGATION Softwood or semi-ripe cuttings in spring or summer; hardwood cuttings in winter; layering in spring

••

GREENFINGER TIP *Practise a regular watering routine during the first year of planting to help it establish successfully, and apply a garden mulch to see it off to a good start*

Jasminum officinale Fiona Sunrise
(also known as 'Frojas')

⬆ 3m/10ft ⬌ 2m/6ft   **EASY**

A relatively new introduction, this deciduous climber has golden-leaved ferny foliage and is absolutely smothered in fragrant white flowers from mid-summer to early autumn. It is average to fast-growing and more compact than other jasmine varieties.

BEST USES Ideal where space is limited, such as in a sunny courtyard garden or on a patio or sheltered roof terrace; the perfume is much stronger in full sun

FLOWERS June to September

SCENTED Yes

ASPECT South or south-west facing, in a sheltered position; full sun to partial shade

SOIL Any fertile, well-drained soil

HARDINESS Frost hardy at temperatures down to -5°C/23°F; may need winter protection in colder areas

DROUGHT TOLERANCE Excellent, once established

PROBLEMS None

PRUNING Cut back lightly after flowering, removing any overcrowded or crossed shoots

PROPAGATION Softwood or semi-ripe cuttings in spring or summer; hardwood cuttings in winter; layering in spring

Jasminum polyanthum 🎖
Many-flowered jasmine

⬆ 3m/10ft ⬌ 2.5m/8ft   **EASY**

One of the easiest jasmines to grow, this really lives up to its common name, producing gorgeous clusters of powerfully scented flowers that are pink in bud and open to pure white. It is evergreen and twining in habit, with pointed green leaves, and flowers from late winter to early spring indoors or in summer outdoors. It produces purple black berries after flowering.

BEST USES Grow against a sheltered, sunny wall in mild areas, up trellis as a fragrant flower screen dividing two garden areas, or to bring an exotic touch to a summer evening in a small city garden

FLOWERS February to April (indoors); June to August (outdoors)

SCENTED Highly fragrant flowers

ASPECT South or west facing, in a sheltered position protected from cold winds; full sun

SOIL Any fertile, well-drained soil

HARDINESS Half hardy at temperatures down to 0°C/32°F; may need winter protection, and best grown in a greenhouse or conservatory in colder areas

DROUGHT TOLERANCE Good, once established

PROBLEMS None outdoors; aphids when under glass

PRUNING Minimal; trim lightly after flowering

PROPAGATION Softwood or semi-ripe cuttings in spring or summer; layering in spring; hardwood cuttings in winter

Lapageria rosea 🎖
Chilean bell flower

⬆ 4m/13ft ⬌ 2.5m/8ft   **EASY**

This is a really easy-to-grow but very exotic-looking evergreen climber from Chile that twines and climbs by suckers, and is best grown on trellis or garden wires from the early stages. It has dark green oval leaves and large, pendent, bell-shaped flowers that are an exquisite rose pink and slightly waxy to the touch, from summer to early autumn.

BEST USES Will climb up trellis or over old tree stumps and low fences, and looks super when grown in containers or against a sheltered brick wall

FLOWERS July to September

SCENTED No

ASPECT North, east or west facing, in a sheltered position; partial to full shade

SOIL Most fertile, well-drained soils; will not tolerate very wet, heavy clay

HARDINESS Frost hardy at temperatures down to -5°C/23°F; may need winter protection, or grow in a greenhouse or conservatory in colder areas

DROUGHT TOLERANCE Poor

PROBLEMS Aphids, mealybug, scale insect and tortrix moth; cold winds can cause leaf damage or loss and prevent the plant establishing

PRUNING None; best left to its own devices

PROPAGATION Sow pre-soaked seed in spring at 13–18°C/55–64°F; layering in spring or autumn

Lathyrus latifolius 🎖
Everlasting sweet pea

⬆ 2.5m/8ft ⬌ 90cm/3ft   **EASY**

Sweet peas always herald the arrival of summer and this delightful herbaceous perennial climber produces dark pink flowers in profusion well into autumn, followed by green pea pods. The leaves are an attractive pale green-grey and it climbs by tendrils. Although this variety is not scented, the abundance of flowers it produces more than makes up for the lack of perfume. Excellent as a cut flower.

BEST USES A great small climber for containers on a sunny patio or growing through shrubs, and an excellent means of clothing the low, bare limbs of shrub roses

FLOWERS July to October

SCENTED No

ASPECT South or west facing, in a sheltered or exposed position; full sun to partial shade

SOIL Any fertile, well-drained soil

HARDINESS Fully hardy at temperatures down to -15°C/5°F; needs no winter protection

DROUGHT TOLERANCE Excellent, once established

PROBLEMS None

PRUNING Cut to ground level in autumn

PROPAGATION Sow pre-soaked seed in a cold frame in spring or autumn

••

GREENFINGER TIP *Pick the flowers regularly to encourage prolonged flowering*

Lathyrus odoratus
Sweet pea

↑ 30–60cm/1–2ft ↔ 30–60cm/1–2ft   **EASY**

This delightful, easy-to-grow annual climber has a long flowering period through to early autumn. The purple-pink flowers are extremely fragrant and produced in abundance, with green pea pods after flowering. The winged leaves are an attractive pale green, and it climbs by tendrils. There are many wonderful varieties and colours to choose from.

BEST USES A great climber for containers, on walls at the back of borders or grown up trellis or brick pillars

FLOWERS July to September
SCENTED Scented flowers
ASPECT South or west facing, in a sheltered or exposed position; full sun to partial shade
SOIL Most fertile, well-drained soils, particularly loam and sand; can tolerate clay if it is not too heavy or waterlogged
HARDINESS Fully hardy at temperatures down to -15°C/5°F; sow seed in final flowering positions in spring, or sow in a cold frame in autumn
DROUGHT TOLERANCE Good, once established
PROBLEMS None
PRUNING None; will die back naturally with the first frosts
PROPAGATION Sow pre-soaked seed in early to mid-spring or mid-autumn to mid-winter, in containers or in situ

....

GREENFINGER TIP Give it a balanced fertiliser once a month during the growing season and keep well watered

Lonicera x brownii 'Dropmore Scarlet'
Scarlet trumpet honeysuckle

↑ 4m/13ft ↔ 2m/6ft   **EASY**

This honeysuckle is semi-evergreen in mild areas but deciduous in colder regions. It is easy to grow, with masses of fragrant, scarlet orange, tubular flowers all the way from June through to September, and attracts hoverflies and bees. It is not as vigorous in habit as some of the other honeysuckles, so ideal where space is restricted, but needs strong support from the start, as it will get weighty in maturity. A real cracker.

BEST USES Ideal subject for the cottage garden, scrambling informally over fences and tree stumps, up the walls of outbuildings and through dull hedging

FLOWERS June to September
SCENTED Scented flowers
ASPECT South or west facing, in a sheltered position; full sun to partial shade
SOIL TYPE Any moist, humus-enriched, well-drained soil
HARDINESS Fully hardy at temperatures down to -15°C/5°F; needs no winter protection
DROUGHT TOLERANCE Good, once established
PROBLEMS Aphids
PRUNING Cut back established plants after flowering, to maintain size and spread, and remove a third of the flowering shoots each year, in late winter or early spring
PROPAGATION Semi-ripe cuttings in summer; greenwood cuttings in summer or hardwood cuttings in autumn; layering in autumn

Rosa Altissimo
(also known as 'Delmur')

⬆ 3m/10ft ⬌ 90cm/3ft   **EASY**

If you like truly red roses, you'll love *Rosa* Altissimo. It's a modern, medium-sized climbing rose, with a fairly stiff habit. The single blooms, approximately 13cm/5in across, are blood red in colour with contrasting bright yellow stamens against shiny dark green foliage, followed by red rose hips. What it lacks in scent it more than makes up for in abundant flowering.

BEST USES Great for containers in a small garden; adapts well to an espaliered treatment against sunny walls at the back of borders, and is a natural choice for growing against trellis or up brick pillars

FLOWERS July to September

SCENTED Slightly scented flowers

ASPECT East, south or west facing, in a sheltered position; full sun to partial shade

SOIL Any fertile, humus-enriched, well-drained soil; also very tolerant of poorer soils

HARDINESS Fully hardy at temperatures down to -15°C/5°F; needs no winter protection

DROUGHT TOLERANCE Excellent, once established

PROBLEMS Aphids; blackspot and powdery mildew

PRUNING Deadhead flowers as they fade and prune out dead, damaged or diseased material; keep an open framework, tying in stems horizontally

PROPAGATION Hardwood cuttings in late autumn

GREENFINGER TIP *Avoid planting in partial shade as this will significantly reduce the number of flowers produced*

Rosa 'Bantry Bay'

⬆ 3.5m/12ft ⬌ 90cm/3ft   **EASY**

A modern, repeat climbing rose that is very free flowering, producing trusses of cupped, lightly scented, bright pink semi-double flowers with yellow stamens, borne in profusion from summer to autumn. It has light green, glossy leaves and is tolerant of north-facing walls and poor soil, as well as being fairly disease resistant.

BEST USES Grow over an arbour, up a pillar or close to the house where you can enjoy the gentle perfume

FLOWERS mid-June for 3–4 weeks, with a second flush in September

SCENTED Lightly scented flowers

ASPECT South or west facing, in a sheltered position; full sun to partial shade

SOIL Any fertile, humus-enriched, well-drained soil

HARDINESS Fully hardy at temperatures down to -15°C/5°F; needs no winter protection

DROUGHT TOLERANCE Excellent, once established

PROBLEMS Aphids; blackspot and powdery mildew

PRUNING Remove dead, damaged or diseased material, and cut back 2–3 stems to 30cm/12in from the base every year in late autumn to early spring

PROPAGATION Hardwood cuttings in late autumn

GREENFINGER TIP *Position this rose in full sun to encourage more profuse flowering*

Climbing roses

Roses are among the most popular plants in the world. From their earliest cultivation by the Greeks and Romans, to the splendours of the royal French gardens and the quaint informal charm of the cottage garden, their infinite variety, colour and perfume have established them in the hearts of gardeners and non-gardeners alike. Who am I to argue with such veneration?

In my own humble view, the reason for the enduring popularity of roses is that they have a very potent thing going for them – romance. Whether tumbling over cottage garden walls, or billowing blowsily around a front porch, they communicate uniquely to the senses. Roses are the only plant I can think of that offer such diversity in flowering shape, habit and an intoxicating array of scents. Everyone has their own special favourites and just the tiniest hint of a particular rose perfume, caught lightly on a summer breeze, can send you reeling wistfully down memory lane. So if you have even the slightest trace of poetry in your soul, there is nothing for it but to plant a climbing rose or two. Garden alchemy.

Cultivation

Roses have a long history and one could devote an entire book to their origins and distinct characteristics. But we are interested here in climbing varieties – which can easily eclipse some of their shrubby forebears with their profuse displays – so let's begin with what must be the most frequently asked question: 'What is the difference between a rambling and a climbing rose?'

The most obvious answer is that climbing roses climb and ramblers, well, ramble, but there are other ways to recognise them.

Ramblers
- tend to have one show of smaller flowers, normally produced in clusters
- put forth new stems annually that will produce next year's flowers
- tend to be more vigorous in their growth and eventual size and are more suitable for covering large walls or buildings, or left to scramble away up a sizeable tree

Climbing roses
- will often produce larger flowers with a second flush of flowering in the same season
- produce fewer stems at the base and the stems themselves tend to be a lot sturdier and less pliable than those of a rambler
- produce new lateral growth along the length of the existing stems
- may be better suited to trellises, pillars, doorways and the like, as they tend to be moderate in their growth habit

When choosing a rose, always consider whether you can provide it with ideal conditions. Although some roses will tolerate shade, most need full sun, so south- or west-facing sites are going to result in more prolific flowering and more perfume, simply because there are more blooms.

Roses are generally easy to grow, preferring rich, loamy soil or clay, though they tend to sulk in very chalky or sandy soil: unless you improve it annually with organic matter they will just look forlorn, grudgingly putting forth some very mean flowers. There is nothing more unattractive than a meagre rose.

The stems of climbing roses tend to be lax, and roses are not self-clinging or self-supporting, so they will need a climbing frame, such as trellis, a pergola or framework of garden wires (see pages 95–7).

When you first buy your rose, it may be growing in a pot or it may be bare-rooted. A bare-rooted rose is one that is delivered to you without a soil ball. It can look pretty unprepossessing, all bare, pruned stems, but the choice of bare-root roses is far wider and normally significantly cheaper than for pot-grown specimens. They are normally dispatched in the months when the plant is dormant, from November to April.

Bare-root specimens can dry out in transit, and it is always wise to soak the roots of any rose thoroughly before planting. The planting process is the same for both container-grown or bare-rooted plants. Dig a good-sized hole (see pages 103–4) – slightly bigger and wider than the size of the pot the rose came in, but not greatly so – and put some well-rotted compost or organic matter straight into the bottom of the planting hole. There is no need to tease out the roots as

Rosa 'Rambling Rector' living up to its name on a pergola

you would with some perennials, though you may spread the roots gently if you wish. Some gardeners advocate lightly pruning the roots of bare-root roses to accelerate the formation of fibrous roots. I'd advise new gardeners to leave well alone, as you may be over-enthusiastic in your root pruning.

You will notice a knobbled growth at the base of the stem, which is known as a 'graft union'. Ensure that this is about 2cm/1in below the soil level when planting. Backfill the hole with soil, firming it to eradicate any potential air pockets and allowing the roots to make good contact with the soil, which will encourage them to establish. It would do no harm to add extra organic mulch around the base of the plant after planting. Tie the stems to their support (see page 43) and, finally, water well.

Pests and diseases

Roses can suffer from 'soil sickness' or 'rose sickness'. This occurs when new roses are planted where old ones used to grow or where other trees and shrubs from the *Rosaceae* family (such as cherries, pears, apples) have previously been grown. Roses suffering from this condition will send out stunted and distorted growth, may fail to flower and, in the worst scenario, just shrivel and die. The only solution is to move your new roses to fresh ground.

'American Pillar' roses clambering over a shed

There are various other maladies that may befall roses, but this doesn't seem to put off the avid rose lover: gardeners will forgive all manner of shortcomings in a rose that they would never tolerate in other garden plants, neatly proving my point that the heart triumphs over old-fashioned common sense every time! Blackspot, rust, mildew and aphids are the most common problems that occur with roses and are very easily dealt with (see pages 109–14). Many roses are now bred to be more disease resistant than their predecessors, so check out the plant's pedigree with your local nursery or garden centre at the time of purchase.

Pruning

Pruning roses always leads to lively debate and most gardeners are brimming with uncertainty as to when, how and why to prune. I was taught to prune to an outward-facing bud, making the cut so that it sloped away from the developing bud, thus channelling rainwater down the opposite side of the stem and allowing the bud to develop without getting excessively wet. Commercial rose growers can't even agree amongst themselves whether pruning their roses individually in this way or shearing them with petrol-powered hedge trimmers will yield the best results, so I can only tell you what has worked successfully in my experience.

There is no need to prune your climbing rose or rambler when it is young and newly planted. In subsequent years, cut back up to a third of the older stems to just above soil level after flowering. At the same time, cut back older flowering side shoots on the remaining plant to within 10cm/4in of the major joint where they join the main stems. Always remove crossed, dead or damaged stems when you prune as a matter of course.

There will come a time, especially with the larger ramblers, when it is practically impossible to prune the top area of a rose as it is just too high and inaccessible, especially if left to grow through a large tree. You can buy long-handled rose loppers with a longer reach, but if the rose is getting on for some 4.5–6m/15–20ft, even these aren't going to have the necessary scope. You try dealing with tree branches and rose stems together – they are a lethal combination! Forget it – do the best you can and don't concern yourself with inaccessible growth.

It may be that removing older stems from the base is the only reasonable way to keep up with pruning a rambling rose, allowing the crop of new, annual, slender basal stems room to develop and encouraging flowering lower down rather than all being up top. Often, the tip of stems that have been pruned die back, perhaps due to frosts, and it may be necessary to prune again to the next 'eyes' or buds lower down. Sometimes a climbing rose puts out lengthy new stems that don't flower at all, normally as a result of weather damage: just cut these back to half their length in the hope that further flowering growth will be stimulated.

Training and feeding

The trick to getting a good climbing rose display lies in training the horizontal stems, as more flowers are produced on stems that grow horizontally. If you establish a good framework of stems right from the start, you can expect more profuse flowering, so it is worth taking the time to train them onto a set of wires or other support.

Your chosen roses will need to be tied in when first planted, and again as they grow, using soft garden twine or plant ties. Climbing roses tend to be sold with longer stems than shrub roses, so simply fan out the

Good companions: sweet peas winding through roses on a metal frame

stems, allowing equal spacing between them, following the natural movement of the plant. Lean the plant towards the support, rather than simply planting it upright as you would most perennials, and tie the stems into the horizontal wires. Most rose stems are slightly stiff and certainly less pliable than other climbers; however, you can gently but firmly bend them onto your wires without splintering.

You will need to leave some vertical stems to produce an even, attractive fan shape, but using this method will prevent all the roses blooming at the top (as is so commonly seen), leaving uninviting, naked stems at the bottom of the plant. The same procedure applies whether you are growing them up a pillar, along a fence or garden wall.

An annual spring-time application of well-rotted manure at the base of your roses is all the feeding they require. It is best not to feed them in late summer or early autumn, as this could prompt the rose to produce new soft growth that may be damaged or killed by the onset of colder weather.

Rosa 'Climbing Cécile Brünner' ♉

↑ 3.5m/12ft ↔ 90cm/3ft   **EASY**

This is a vigorous climber with dark green leaves, though the leaf coverage is fairly sparse. It is from China rose stock and is much loved for its airy sprays of perfectly shaped, fragrant, small, rosebud-pink double flowers. It flowers continuously from summer to autumn and has the further advantage of being almost thornless.

BEST USES Will grow well through trees, as it is fairly vigorous, but looks equally at home in the cottage garden or against a courtyard wall

FLOWERS July to September

SCENTED Lightly scented flowers

ASPECT Any, in a sheltered position; full sun

SOIL Any fertile, humus-enriched, well-drained soil

HARDINESS Fully hardy at temperatures down to -15°C/5°F; needs no winter protection

DROUGHT TOLERANCE Excellent, once established

PROBLEMS Aphids; blackspot and powdery mildew

PRUNING Remove dead, damaged or diseased material, and cut back 2–3 stems to 30cm/12in from the base every year in late autumn to early spring

PROPAGATION Hardwood cuttings in late autumn

....

GREENFINGER TIP *This rose needs the sunniest position for the best show of flowers, but will also perform adequately on a north-facing wall*

Rosa 'Climbing Iceberg' ♉

↑ 4m/13ft ↔ 4m/13ft   **EASY**

'Climbing Iceberg' is a reliable, trouble-free mainstay rose that suffers less from maladies than others of its kind. My daughter bought me one from Woolworth's years ago and it's still going strong. It has glossy green leaves and large, white, fragrant flowers in summer and autumn, which are pretty weather resistant.

BEST USES Particularly useful for small courtyards, wall-side borders and container gardens

FLOWERS June to September

SCENTED Lightly scented flowers

ASPECT East, south or west facing, in a sheltered position; full sun

SOIL Any fertile, well-drained soil

HARDINESS Fully hardy at temperatures down to -15°C/5°F; needs no winter protection

DROUGHT TOLERANCE Excellent, once established

PROBLEMS Aphids; blackspot and rose rust; rabbits

PRUNING Minimal; cut out damaged stems in late autumn to early spring

PROPAGATION Hardwood cuttings in late autumn

....

GREENFINGER TIP *This rose is easy to grow and its blooms resist rose ball even in very wet weather*

Rosa 'Constance Spry'

↑ 2m/6ft ↔ 2m/6ft   **EASY**

'Ah, dear old Connie Spry' is an exclamation often heard in reference to this well-behaved, David Austin, modern shrub rose that bears large, old-fashioned double, clear pink blooms on nodding stems. The flower displays are sumptuous and possess a heavenly myrrh-like fragrance, making it deservedly one of the most popular climbing roses around. It has an informal, lax habit, so is best tied in to a strong framework from the outset.

BEST USES Site on a sunny wall in a seating area where you can appreciate the fragrance; also looks charming trained over low walls or up brick pillars

FLOWERS July to September
SCENTED Scented flowers
ASPECT Any, in a sheltered position; full sun to partial shade
SOIL Any fertile, humus-enriched, well-drained soil
HARDINESS Fully hardy at temperatures down to -15°C/5°F; needs no winter protection
DROUGHT TOLERANCE Excellent, once established
PROBLEMS Aphids; powdery mildew
PRUNING Remove dead, damaged or diseased material and cut back 2–3 stems to 30cm/12in from the base every year in late autumn to early spring
PROPAGATION Hardwood cuttings in late autumn

Rosa 'Gloire de Dijon'
Old glory rose

↑ 4m/13ft ↔ 2.5m/8ft   **EASY**

A popular and vigorous climbing tea rose that has attractive, glossy dark green leaves and gorgeously crumpled, creamy yellow-white double flowers that are lightly tipped with pink, as well as a full, spicy scent. It's a loose, free-flowering, romantic-looking rose, and really worth growing for its heavenly perfume and repeat flowering throughout summer and early autumn. Rose growers would almost universally vote this as one of the all-time greats.

BEST USES Plant where the fragrance can be appreciated; its informal habit suits a cottage garden

FLOWERS July to September
SCENTED Richly scented flowers
ASPECT Any, in a sheltered position; full sun to partial shade
SOIL Any fertile, humus-enriched, well-drained soil
HARDINESS Fully hardy at temperatures down to -15°C/5°F; needs no winter protection
DROUGHT TOLERANCE Excellent, once established
PROBLEMS Aphids; blackspot, powdery mildew and rust; dislikes very wet weather, when the buds spoil
PRUNING Remove dead, damaged or diseased material and cut back 2–3 stems to 30cm/12in from the base every year in late autumn to early spring
PROPAGATION Hardwood cuttings in late autumn

GREENFINGER TIP *It can be leggy at the bottom, so grow in a border, where perennials will hide the bare stems*

Rosa 'Golden Showers' ♊

⬆ 3.5m/12ft ↔ 2.5m/8ft   **EASY**

I am told this is one of the best-selling yellow climbing roses, and it is not difficult to see why. It is a strong climbing rose of fairly stiff, upright habit, bearing clusters of large, fragrant, golden yellow flowers that fade to pale cream as they age. The leaves are an attractive, glossy dark green and the thorns aren't too abundant, which makes tying it in to its supports easier.

BEST USES With its rather upright habit, this is ideal to grow on trellis or tied in against a sunny wall, and for covering small or courtyard garden walls; a natural choice for wildlife or cottage gardens, as pollinating insects love the flowers

FLOWERS July to September

SCENTED Scented flowers

ASPECT East, south or west facing, in a sheltered position; full sun

SOIL Any fertile, humus-enriched, well-drained soil

HARDINESS Fully hardy at temperatures down to -15°C/5°F; needs no winter protection

DROUGHT TOLERANCE Excellent, once established

PROBLEMS Aphids; blackspot and powdery mildew

PRUNING Remove dead, damaged or diseased material and cut back 2–3 stems to 30cm/12in from the base every year in late autumn to early spring

PROPAGATION Hardwood cuttings in late autumn

Rosa 'New Dawn' ♊

⬆ 3m/10ft ↔ 2m/6ft   **EASY**

A popular, reliable, bushy, repeat rambling rose that has mid-green leaves and clusters of fragrant, double, pale ice-pink flowers produced throughout the summer and often well into autumn. I've even caught it throwing out isolated new blooms in November! It has good disease resistance, and is able to thrive in light shade, so well worth trying on a north-facing wall – though in truth it flowers best in full sun.

BEST USES Grow over an arch or against a warm sunny wall; also ideal for shady city courtyards

FLOWERS June to October

SCENTED Highly scented flowers

ASPECT Any, in a sheltered position; full sun to partial shade

SOIL Any fertile, humus-enriched, well-drained soil

HARDINESS Fully hardy at temperatures down to -15°C/5°F; needs no winter protection

DROUGHT TOLERANCE Excellent, once established

PROBLEMS Aphids; powdery mildew

PRUNING Cut back old flowering side shoots once flowering is over to approximately 10cm/4in from the main stems; if plant is very mature, just cut old flower stems to ground level after flowering, and remove dead, damaged or diseased material

PROPAGATION Hardwood cuttings in late autumn

Rosa Warm Welcome ♟
(also known as 'Chewizz')

↑ 2m/6ft ↔ 2.5m/8ft **EASY**

This deserves a mention because I can't think of too many roses that give such a willing, reliable and prolonged flowering display that repeats throughout the summer. It may not be to everyone's taste with its abundant, bold clusters of flame-orange flowers, but this modern climbing rose with semi-evergreen leaves, offsetting the furious orange blooms, is very eye-catching.

BEST USES Ideal trained up pillars or for containers on the patio, bringing hot, exotic colour into a lightly shaded courtyard or city garden and it can really brighten up a north-facing wall

FLOWERS June to October
SCENTED No
ASPECT Any, in a sheltered position; full sun to partial shade
SOIL Any fertile, well-drained soil
HARDINESS Fully hardy at temperatures down to -15°C/5°F; needs no winter protection
DROUGHT TOLERANCE Excellent, once established
PROBLEMS Aphids; blackspot and rust
PRUNING Minimal; cut out damaged stems in late autumn to early spring
PROPAGATION Hardwood cuttings in late autumn

....
GREENFINGER TIP *This rose is easy to grow and has a repeat flowering habit from summer to autumn, so is well worth trying. Be bold!*

Stephanotis floribunda ♟
Bridal wreath

↑ 3m/10ft ↔ 3m/10ft **MEDIUM**

A tender, evergreen twining climber producing heavy trusses of pure white, waxy tubular flowers, set against handsome, leathery oval leaves. Greenish oblong fruits are produced after flowering. Needs to be tied in to a sturdy support.

BEST USES Grow as a house plant or in a conservatory; can be placed outside in the summer months

FLOWERS May to October (indoors); June to August (outdoors)
SCENTED Highly fragrant flowers
ASPECT Indoors, in a north- or east-facing window, in a light spot but shielded from direct sunlight; outdoors, west- or south-west facing, sheltered from winds with shade from midday sun
SOIL Any moist, fertile, humus-rich, well-drained soil
HARDINESS Tender; not hardy at temperatures below 15°C/59°F; grow in a greenhouse or conservatory
DROUGHT TOLERANCE Poor
PROBLEMS Mealybug, red spider mite, scale insect and whitefly, when grown in a greenhouse or conservatory
PRUNING In late winter or early spring, remove any dead or damaged foliage and stems; prune lightly after flowering to maintain size and shape
PROPAGATION Sow seed in spring at 18–21°C/64–70°F; semi-ripe cuttings with bottom heat and provide shade

....
GREENFINGER TIP *When grown indoors, mist the leaves regularly with a water spray and keep the soil moist, giving a liquid feed at three-weekly intervals; reduce watering in winter, keeping the soil nearly dry to the touch*

Tropaeolum majus 'African Queen'
Nasturtium

⬆ 30cm/12in ⬌ 45cm/18in EASY

Oh how I love nasturtiums! It is their very gaucheness that makes them so appealing. Although they aren't technically climbing plants, they will tangle themselves through the lower limbs of other climbers rather charmingly and are easy-peasy to grow as annuals. This variety has cheery red and orange flowers with marbled light green foliage. ('Empress of India' is a stunning red variety.)

BEST USES Grow them up a low fence, pop them in hanging baskets or containers, or let them loose in the herbaceous border

FLOWERS June to October

SCENTED No

ASPECT South or west facing, in a sheltered position; full sun

SOIL Any reasonable to poor garden soil

HARDINESS Frost tender, not hardy at temperatures below 3°C/37°F; best grown as an annual

DROUGHT TOLERANCE Poor

PROBLEMS Cabbage white caterpillars; slugs and snails

PRUNING None; will die back with the first frosts

PROPAGATION Sow annual seed in mid-spring to early summer at 13–16°C/55–61°F, in situ

• •

GREENFINGER TIP *In milder areas these will survive moderate winters, and they also self-seed freely: their offspring put on a gaudy show year after year without the need for re-sowing, even in my garden in cold East Anglia*

Actinidia kolomikta 🎖
Kolomikta vine

⬆ 5m/16ft ⬌ 1.5–2m/5–6ft EASY

A really striking, vigorous deciduous climber which requires firm support in early growth, grown mainly for its 15cm/6in long pointed leaves that have cream tips in spring, ageing to pink in more mature plants in summer. The insignificant round white flowers have a light fragrance. Yellow fruits are produced in autumn.

BEST USES Looks spectacular climbing up large trees; particularly effective against a sunny wall or side of the house

FLOWERS June to August, but grown mainly for summer foliage

SCENTED Lightly scented flowers

ASPECT South or west facing, in a sheltered position; full sun

SOIL Any free-draining soil

HARDINESS Fully hardy at temperatures down to -15°C/23°F; needs protection from cold winds

DROUGHT TOLERANCE Poor

PROBLEMS None

PRUNING Cut out any crossed, diseased or overcrowded stems in early spring and tie the main stems onto horizontal wires

PROPAGATION Sow seed in spring or autumn; greenwood or semi-ripe cuttings in early summer; hardwood cuttings in late autumn to mid-winter; layering in autumn

• •

GREENFINGER TIP *Cats love this plant, so protect growing stems from their claws and teeth*

Ampelopsis brevipedunculata var. *maximowiczii* 'Elegans'

⬆ 5m/16ft ⬌ 90cm/3ft **MEDIUM**

This vine-like deciduous climber has a moderate growth habit and attractive, palm-shaped, mottled pink and cream variegated leaves with pinkish tendrils, first appearing in spring. The small green flowers are insignificant, but grape-like clusters of pinky turquoise-coloured berries are produced in late summer to early autumn.

BEST USES Grow in a warm conservatory, cool greenhouse or against a warm sheltered wall; also great for growing in containers where space is limited

FLOWERS Insignificant; grown mainly for summer foliage and autumn berries

SCENTED No

ASPECT Any, in a sheltered position; full sun to partial shade, though best berry colour is achieved in full sun

SOIL Most moist, fertile, well-drained soils, but prefers chalky acidic soil; add peat when planting in other soils to help it establish

HARDINESS Borderline, frost hardy at temperatures down to -5°C/23°F; needs winter protection

DROUGHT TOLERANCE Poor

PROBLEMS Red spider mite when grown under glass; mildew

PRUNING Remove faded leaves and stems in autumn; will die back naturally with the first frosts

PROPAGATION Sow seed in autumn; softwood cuttings or greenwood cuttings in early and mid-summer; hardwood cuttings in winter

Clematis x *triternata* 'Rubromarginata' ▯

⬆ 4.5m/15ft ⬌ 2.5m/8ft **EASY**

A vigorous deciduous climber that bears masses of tiny, spidery, four-sepalled scented flowers in rosy purple hues with whitish central streaks, from summer to early autumn. The almond-like perfume is nothing short of sublime, and the tactile silky seed heads are an added bonus. It was always a well-kept secret among plantsmen but is more widely available now, and well worth the hunt.

BEST USES One of the best climbers to grow over shrubs or small trees as it never matures to a size where its weight will burden its companion plant

FLOWERS July to September

SCENTED Scented flowers

ASPECT Any, in a sheltered or exposed position; full sun to light shade

SOIL Any fertile, well-drained soil

HARDINESS Fully hardy at temperatures down to -15°C/5°F; needs no winter protection

DROUGHT TOLERANCE Poor

PROBLEMS Aphids, caterpillars and earwigs; clematis wilt

PRUNING Cut back to a pair of strong healthy buds about 15cm/6in above ground level before growth starts in spring (Group 3)

PROPAGATION Internodal semi-ripe cuttings in mid to late summer; layering late summer to early autumn

Clematis vitalba
Old man's beard/Traveller's joy

⬆ 5m/16ft ⬌ 1.5–2m/5–6ft   **EASY**

A deciduous, vigorous, fast-growing native climber that is easy to care for. It is smothered with flowers that smell faintly of vanilla in the summer months. The flowers are creamy white tinged with green, and are followed by attractive whiskery seed heads in autumn.

BEST USES Ideal for covering outbuildings, as it has a rapid growth rate; useful for growing over large spring-flowering shrubs, which will support its weight easily, to extend the period of flowering interest

FLOWERS June to September
SCENTED Lightly fragrant flowers
ASPECT South or west facing, in a sheltered position; full sun to partial shade
SOIL Any fertile, well-drained soil
HARDINESS Fully hardy at temperatures down to -15°C/5°F; needs no winter protection
DROUGHT TOLERANCE Poor
PROBLEMS Clematis wilt
PRUNING Minimal; trim lightly after flowering to maintain shape and size (Group 1)
PROPAGATION Internodal semi-ripe cuttings in mid to late summer; layering late summer to early autumn

••

GREENFINGER TIP *The base of this clematis can become bare and straggly, with flowers only being produced higher up. To achieve flowering lower down, cut back all stems to approximately 30cm/12in above ground level in early spring*

Fremontodendron 'California Glory' 🎖
Flannel flower

⬆ 8m/26ft ⬌ 4m/13ft   **EASY**

Sometimes my own prejudices make it hard to do a plant justice: I'm afraid that the flannel flower is one of those. It is a very vigorous evergreen shrub that has bright yellow flowers over a long flowering period, from late spring to autumn. The lobed leaves are fairly attractive but have hairy undersides which can be irritating to skin. Purple black berries are produced in autumn.

BEST USES An extremely vigorous climber for south- and west-facing walls or large outbuildings; growing it in a container may restrain its loutish tendencies

FLOWERS May to October
SCENTED No
ASPECT South or west facing, in a sheltered position; full sun
SOIL Any fertile, well-drained soil
HARDINESS Frost hardy at temperatures down to -5°C/23°F; may require winter protection
DROUGHT TOLERANCE Good, once established
PROBLEMS Prone to root disease
PRUNING Best left to go its own way and, frankly, it rampages away leaving very little choice in the matter!
PROPAGATION Sow seed in spring at 13–18°C/55–64°F; semi-ripe cuttings in late summer; hardwood cuttings in late autumn to late winter

••

GREENFINGER TIP *It's a brute of potentially monstrous proportions, and invades poor mortar joints, so only situate on a sound wall. Fortunately, this plant can be very short-lived (there is a God after all!)*

Hoya carnosa ♎
Wax plant

⬆ 8m/26ft ⬌ 1.2–1.5m/4–5ft   **MEDIUM**

Here's a slightly unusual, succulent evergreen twiner from Asia and Australia that is best grown indoors as a greenhouse or conservatory plant. It has dark green leaves and large, incredibly fragrant flower heads, made up of myriad star-shaped pale pink flowers, with reddish eyes. The scent is strongest at night.

BEST USES Especially good in a conservatory adjoining a dining area, where you can really appreciate the night fragrance

FLOWERS May to September

SCENTED Night-scented flowers

ASPECT South or west facing, in a sheltered position (outdoors); better grown as a houseplant in a bright spot, out of direct sunlight

SOIL All fertile, well-drained soils

HARDINESS Frost tender, not hardy at temperatures below 5°C/41°F; needs indoor protection

DROUGHT TOLERANCE Poor

PROBLEMS Mealybug when grown indoors

PRUNING Minimal; pinch out new shoots, but leave the obviously stubby spurs well alone as these will form flowers for the following year

PROPAGATION Semi-ripe cuttings at any time (minimum temperature 20°C/68°F); layering at any time

GREENFINGER TIP *Water well during flowering but maintain a drier regime when the plant is not flowering, letting the soil almost dry out between watering*

Humulus lupulus 'Aureus' ♎
Golden hop

⬆ 8m/26ft ⬌ 2.5m/8ft   **EASY**

A vigorous, herbaceous twining climber that has large, yellow-gold palm-shaped leaves and is one of the most gratifying plants to grow. Its green to yellow flowers are lightly fragrant, and are followed by pendent, golden, buff-brown hops in autumn. This glorious informal climber rates 9/10 for foliage, visual impact and ease: it's a stunning plant.

BEST USES Lovely grown over a large pergola or used as a foliage screen

FLOWERS July to August, but grown mainly for summer foliage and autumn hops

SCENTED Lightly scented flowers

ASPECT East, south or west facing, in a sheltered position; full sun to partial shade

SOIL Any moist, fertile, humus-rich, well-drained soil

HARDINESS Fully hardy at temperatures down to -15°C/5°F; needs no winter protection

DROUGHT TOLERANCE Poor

PROBLEMS Aphids and caterpillars; powdery mildew

PRUNING Cut back hard to ground level in late winter or early spring (though it looks lovely covered by a hard frost, so perhaps wait until spring?)

PROPAGATION Leaf-bud cuttings in spring to early summer; layering in spring

GREENFINGER TIP *This climber grows fairly rapidly in a year, so make sure you give it plenty of space*

Jasminum x *stephanense*

⬆ 5m/16ft ⬅➡ 90cm/3ft   **EASY**

A delicate, summer-flowering deciduous climber of twining habit, with clusters of sweetly fragrant, pale pink star-shaped flowers, offset by leaves that are pale yellow when young, maturing to green. Although not as vigorous as other jasmine varieties, it should appeal to gardeners with limited outdoor space. The scent is undoubtedly stronger when planted in full sun.

BEST USES Site near seating areas and paths so its sweet fragrance may be fully appreciated

FLOWERS June to July

SCENTED Scented flowers

ASPECT South or west facing, in a sheltered position; full sun to partial shade

SOIL Any fertile, well-drained soil

HARDINESS Frost hardy to -5°C/23°F; needs winter protection in colder areas

DROUGHT TOLERANCE Poor

PROBLEMS None

PRUNING Remove dead or damaged stems after flowering

PROPAGATION Softwood or semi-ripe cuttings in spring or summer; hardwood cuttings in winter; layering in spring

Plumbago auriculata ♀

Cape leadwort

⬆ 5m/16ft ⬅➡ 2.5m/8ft   **EASY**

A South African scrambling shrub that has abundant, dainty, very pretty heads of pure sky blue flowers from summer to late autumn and fresh, light green oval leaves. The sticky seeds get everywhere, but it is such a delight that this hardly matters. It uses other plants as supports, so it will need a trellis or bamboo framework if grown in isolation.

BEST USES Ideal for growing in containers in sheltered hot, sunny courtyards, patios or roof terraces, or in a conservatory; also fairly tolerant of salt-laden coastal winds, if given shelter

FLOWERS June to November

SCENTED No

ASPECT South or west facing, in a sheltered position; full sun

SOIL Light, well-drained soil

HARDINESS Half hardy at temperatures down to 0°C/32°F; needs winter protection, or overwinter in a frost-free greenhouse or conservatory

DROUGHT TOLERANCE Poor

PROBLEMS Aphids

PRUNING Cut back hard in April and it will send up plentiful new shoots in no time

PROPAGATION Sow seed in spring at 13–18°C/ 55–64°F; softwood or semi-ripe stem cuttings with bottom heat in spring to summer

GREENFINGER TIP *Tie in new shoots and give it a proprietary feed once a month in the growing season*

Rosa 'Albéric Barbier'

4.5m/15ft ↔ 2m/6ft EASY

A justifiably popular, energetic, semi-evergreen rambling rose bearing a joyful profusion of trusses of heavily perfumed, creamy white flower clusters in early summer, with appealing, glossy dark green leaves. The clean, fresh perfume is a blend of lemons and apples, and small, oval, orange hips follow the flowers.

BEST USES Will grow well through trees, over a large run of trellis or tied in against a sunny wall; looks marvellous left to grow up the side of a building in wild exuberance; does well on a north-facing wall

FLOWERS June to July
SCENTED Scented flowers
ASPECT Any, in a sheltered or exposed position; full sun to partial shade
SOIL Any fertile, humus-enriched, well-drained soil
HARDINESS Fully hardy at temperatures down to -15°C/5°F; needs no winter protection
DROUGHT TOLERANCE Excellent, once established
PROBLEMS Aphids; blackspot and powdery mildew
PRUNING Ramblers can be difficult to prune because of their size in maturity; if you can reach, remove dead, damaged or diseased material, trim the tips of new shoots to encourage flowering, and tie in new growth
PROPAGATION Hardwood cuttings in late autumn

Rosa 'Albertine'

4.5m/15ft ↔ 2m/6ft EASY

An enduringly popular, vigorous rambling rose with mid-green, fairly dense leaves, which are reddish when young and display the bronze pink-toned rose buds exceptionally well. The buds develop into fragrant, loose, blowsy blooms of coppery pink. However, it is too prone to mildew for my taste!

BEST USES Leave to its own devices, scrambling up a large tree, over arches, hedges and outbuildings, or tie in to a large trellis or garden walkway

FLOWERS June to July
SCENTED Scented flowers
ASPECT East, south or west facing, in a sheltered position; full sun
SOIL Any fertile, humus-enriched, well-drained soil
HARDINESS Fully hardy at temperatures down to -15°C/5°F; needs no winter protection
DROUGHT TOLERANCE Excellent, once established
PROBLEMS Aphids; blackspot, powdery mildew and rust
PRUNING Prune about a third of the older stems to ground level to encourage new growth at the top, and tie in new stems; cut back old flowering side shoots once flowering is over to about 10cm/4in from the main stems
PROPAGATION Hardwood cuttings in late autumn

GREENFINGER TIP *In extremely wet weather, the flower buds turn brown and hang forlornly on the plant, spoilt for that season – you will just have to cut them off*

Rosa 'American Pillar'

⬆ 5m/16ft ↔ 2m/6ft   **EASY**

A vigorous rambling rose with glossy dark green leaves and clusters of single and double flowers that some call carmine red, but I would say are brash reddy pink. The extravagant blooms have white centres and vivid yellow stamens. Though the scent is hardly discernible, I love this rose – it's so extrovert and exuberant in its flower power, and stands up to wind and rain very well.

BEST USES Will grow well through trees, over trellis or tied in against a sunny wall

FLOWERS June

SCENTED Faintly scented flowers

ASPECT East, south or west facing, in a sheltered position; full sun

SOIL Any fertile, humus-enriched, well-drained soil

HARDINESS Fully hardy at temperatures down to -15°C/5°F; needs no winter protection

DROUGHT TOLERANCE Excellent, once established

PROBLEMS Aphids; blackspot and powdery mildew

PRUNING Ramblers can be difficult to prune because of their size in maturity; if you can reach, remove dead, damaged or diseased material, trim the tips of new shoots to encourage flowering, and tie in new growth

PROPAGATION Hardwood cuttings in late autumn

GREENFINGER TIP *I have grown this planted in 6m/20ft of sandy soil and never once had to water it. I'd say its drought tolerance is excellent, but others report less tolerance. You'll have to make up your own mind!*

Rosa 'Crimson Glory Climbing'

⬆ 4.5m/15ft ↔ 2m/6ft   **EASY**

This climbing version of the Hybrid Tea bush rose 'Crimson Glory' has velvety, deep crimson semi-double flowers with golden stamens and the most exquisite perfume. The leaves are a deep, glossy green that shows off the summer blooms to great advantage. It's the sort of 'proper' rose I remember from my grandad's garden – it smells and looks just as a rose should.

BEST USES Grow against a sunny wall or around an arbour in a prominent position, so that you get a heady draught of its rich perfume

FLOWERS July, with a second flush in September

SCENTED Highly scented flowers

ASPECT South or west facing, in a sheltered position; full sun

SOIL Any fertile, humus-enriched, well-drained soil

HARDINESS Fully hardy at temperatures down to -15°C/5°F; needs no winter protection

DROUGHT TOLERANCE Excellent, once established

PROBLEMS Aphids; blackspot and powdery mildew

PRUNING Remove dead, damaged or diseased material or excessive growth at any time; once established, flowering side shoots can be pruned back to a third of their length in late autumn to winter

PROPAGATION Hardwood cuttings in late autumn

Rosa 'Rambling Rector' ♀

⬆ 8m/26ft ⬌ 4m/12ft   **EASY**

This charming old cleric is a vigorous grower, producing sprays of small, perfumed, creamy white semi-double flowers with attractive yellow centres throughout the summer, followed by oval orange hips in autumn. It is commonly seen rambling over hedges and scrambling in its blowsy manner over outhouses in country gardens.

BEST USES Grow over a large arbour or use to clothe a sizeable outbuilding or garage: it gets big, so allow plenty of room

FLOWERS July to September

SCENTED Highly scented flowers

ASPECT East, south or west facing, in an exposed or sheltered position; full sun

SOIL Any fertile, humus-enriched, well-drained soil

HARDINESS Fully hardy at temperatures down to -15°C/5°F; needs no winter protection

DROUGHT TOLERANCE Excellent, once established

PROBLEMS Aphids; blackspot, powdery mildew and rust

PRUNING Cut back old flowering side shoots once flowering is over to about 10cm/4in from the main stems; if plant is very mature, just cut old flower stems to ground level after flowering, and remove dead, damaged or diseased material

PROPAGATION Hardwood cuttings in late autumn

GREENFINGER TIP *This rose really needs the sunniest position for the best profusion of flowers, but it will do reasonably well on a north-facing wall*

Trachelospermum jasminoides ♀
Confederate jasmine

⬆ 8m/26ft ⬌ 8m/26ft   **EASY**

An evergreen twining climber with glossy dark green leaves that turn a delightful wine colour in autumn. The real wow factor is the mass of highly perfumed, small, pure white star-shaped flowers from mid to late summer. The scent is stronger in the evening, attracting night-pollinating insects, and it brings a touch of exotic luxury to any garden.

BEST USES Excellent for introducing scented glamour into courtyards, city gardens or roof terraces and in warm sunny borders at the foot of a sheltered south-facing wall

FLOWERS July to August

SCENTED Highly scented flowers

ASPECT South or west facing, in a sheltered position; full sun

SOIL Any fertile, well-drained soil

HARDINESS Frost hardy at temperatures down to -5°C/23°F; may need winter protection; in colder areas, move plants in containers to a frost-free spot in winter

DROUGHT TOLERANCE Poor

PROBLEMS None outdoors; mealybug and red spider mite when grown indoors

PRUNING Minimal; trim lightly in early spring to retain its size and shape

PROPAGATION Semi-ripe cuttings with bottom heat in summer or layering in autumn

Actinidia deliciosa
Kiwi fruit/Chinese gooseberry

⬆ 10m/32ft ↔ 1.5–2m/5–6ft   **EASY**

The kiwi fruit is a woody-stemmed deciduous vine, with large, heart-shaped leaves. The young shoots and leaves are covered with red hairs and the white flowers are fragrant, maturing to a pale yellow. A very attractive ornamental climber for garden use, it is grown commercially for its crop of large, hairy, egg-shaped fruits, with bright green fleshy interiors. Although there is a self-fertile variety, 'Jenny', both male and female plants are usually needed for fruit production.

BEST USES Great as an ornamental climber trained on wires against a warm, sheltered wall, and an excellent foliage plant in a walled kitchen garden

FLOWERS June to August, but grown mainly for foliage

SCENTED Scented flowers

ASPECT South or west facing, in a sheltered position with protection from cold winds; full sun

SOIL Any fertile, humus-enriched, well-drained soil

HARDINESS Frost hardy at temperatures down to -5°C/23°F; spring frosts will damage flowering wood

DROUGHT TOLERANCE Poor

PROBLEMS Prone to root rot; needs full sun to fruit

PRUNING When new leaf buds begin to develop in spring, prune out old or damaged wood

PROPAGATION Sow seed in spring or autumn; greenwood or semi-ripe cuttings in summer; hardwood cuttings in late autumn or mid-winter; layering in autumn

Araujia sericifera
Cruel plant

⬆ 10m/32ft ↔ 3m/10ft   **TRICKY**

This is an unusual, evergreen, woody-stemmed twining climber, originally from South America. It has grey-green leaves that are downy white underneath, and oddly scented (some would say disagreeable), funnel-shaped white flowers, often streaked with pale pink on the insides, in late summer. Large green pods are produced, particularly after long, hot summers. It will need support from an early stage.

BEST USES An ideal climber for containers for hot, sunny patios; will tolerate partial shade in frost-free areas, but in cold regions is best grown as a conservatory plant

FLOWERS July to August

SCENTED Scented flowers

ASPECT East, south or west facing, in a sheltered position; full sun to partial shade

SOIL Any fertile, well-drained soil

HARDINESS Half hardy at temperatures down to 0°C/32°F; will need winter protection

DROUGHT TOLERANCE Poor

PROBLEMS Red spider mite when grown indoors

PRUNING Minimal; trim after flowering to restrict its height and spread to the available space

PROPAGATION Sow seed in spring or when ripe; semi-ripe cuttings of lateral shoots with bottom heat in summer

Aristolochia macrophylla
(formerly *A. durior*) Dutchman's pipe

⬆ 12m/40ft ↔ 4m/13ft   **EASY**

A vigorous deciduous twining vine, largely grown for its broad, deeply veined, kidney-shaped foliage, which offers a pleasing contrast to the mature, tactile, corky stem. Unusual, mottled maroon or greeny purple saxophone-shaped flowers are almost hidden in the leaves, but they are definitely a curiosity. This exotic-looking climber can reach a great height in a relatively short period of time, and it is a real eye-catcher.

BEST USES Good for pillars, pergolas or covering trellis and walls; ideal for regions with hot summers and cold winters

FLOWERS June, but grown mainly for foliage
SCENTED No
ASPECT East, south or west facing, in a sheltered position protected from winds; full sun to partial shade
SOIL Any moist, fertile, well-drained soil; plants grown in drier soils overwinter better than those in wetter soils
HARDINESS Frost hardy at temperatures down to -5°C/23°F; needs winter protection in colder areas
DROUGHT TOLERANCE Poor
PROBLEMS None
PRUNING Cut back hard in late winter, when dormant; pinch out new growth in the growing season to encourage dense foliage cover
PROPAGATION Sow seed in spring; greenwood cuttings in spring

Jasminum officinale ♀
Common jasmine

⬆ 12m/40ft ↔ 3m/10ft   **EASY**

This is a popular, easy, fast-growing deciduous climber with small, green, pointed leaves that will remain semi-evergreen in warmer regions and has a twining habit. But it is the clusters of small, highly fragrant, star-shaped flowers, pinkish in bud and opening to pure white, that are its claim to fame – and justifiably so. It will need support from the early stages, as it is potentially a large climber.

BEST USES Particularly good for sheltered sunny gardens and patios, scrambling through trees or on roof terraces (with shelter from winds)

FLOWERS June to August
SCENTED Highly fragrant flowers
ASPECT South or west facing, in a sheltered position; full sun to partial shade
SOIL Most moist, fertile, well-drained soils, though not heavy, poorly drained clay
HARDINESS Frost hardy to temperatures of -5°C/23°F; needs winter protection in cold areas
DROUGHT TOLERANCE Excellent, once established
PROBLEMS Aphids
PRUNING Trim lightly after flowering to restrict its size and shape
PROPAGATION Softwood or semi-ripe cuttings in spring or summer; hardwood cuttings in winter; layering in spring

Lonicera japonica
Japanese honeysuckle

⬆ 10m/32ft ⬌ 2m/6ft **EASY**

This evergreen honeysuckle is easy to grow, though more slow-growing than others of its kind. It has scented, creamy to pale yellow flowers from early summer into autumn, followed by dark blue berries. The scent is stronger in the evenings. It should be given strong support, such as a wall or fence, from the start, as the leaf mass is potentially very heavy.

BEST USES Will scramble happily over fences, old tree stumps or to add rustic charm to tatty outbuildings or severe modern garages; delightful trained over a garden walkway in a cottage garden

FLOWERS June to September
SCENTED Scented flowers
ASPECT Any, in a sheltered or exposed position; full sun to partial shade
SOIL Rich, moist, humus-enriched, well-drained soil
HARDINESS Fully hardy at temperatures down to -15°C/5°F; needs no winter protection
DROUGHT TOLERANCE Good, once established
PROBLEMS Aphids
PRUNING Cut back established plants after flowering, removing a third of the flowering shoots
PROPAGATION Softwood or semi-ripe cuttings in spring to late summer; hardwood cuttings in late autumn to mid-winter; layering in spring

Passiflora caerulea 🎖
Passionflower

⬆ 10m/32ft ⬌ 10m/32ft **EASY**

This popular evergreen climber clings by tendrils that look delicate, but don't be deceived. It has abundant, unusual and incredibly graphic white flowers with bluey purple-fringed filaments that are at their best from late summer, and shiny, deep green, lobed leaves. Exotic-looking yet surprisingly trouble free, it is vigorous and thrives in hot summers, producing attractive orange fruits after flowering that are edible but not tasty.

BEST USES Great for the cottage garden, and a really lavish sight left to cover a tall brick wall

FLOWERS July to September
SCENTED No
ASPECT South or west facing, in a sheltered position; full sun, though tolerates partial shade
SOIL Well-drained, fertile, moist, light soils such as loam or sand; will do reasonably well in clay and chalk
HARDINESS Half hardy at temperatures down to 0°C/32°F; needs winter protection
DROUGHT TOLERANCE Excellent, once established
PROBLEMS None
PRUNING Cut out dead or damaged material in early spring; cut back flowering shoots after the flowers fade to 2–3 buds of the structured framework
PROPAGATION Sow seed at any time; semi-ripe cuttings in summer or autumn; layering in spring

....

GREENFINGER TIP *Established plants will tolerate frosts: though the top-growth may be damaged by cold and frost, it will inevitably shoot back again in spring*

Rosa filipes 'Kiftsgate' ♀

⬆ 10m/32ft ↔ 6m/20ft   **EASY**

A lovely, but very vigorous, perfumed rambling rose with scented sprays of single, creamy white flowers with yellow eyes in summer. Though the flowers are small, the flower production is generous, which more than makes up for their size. It is potentially a very large climber, so site it where you can allow it plenty of space when initially choosing its planting position. It needs strong supports, unless it is grown up a large tree which is more than man enough to cope.

BEST USES A heavenly rose that is potentially of great size – mine's reached nearly 15m/50ft! – but a fantastic sight when in full flower climbing up a large tree or over a tall garden wall or large outbuilding

FLOWERS July to August
SCENTED Lightly scented flowers
ASPECT East, south or west facing, in a sheltered or exposed position; full sun
SOIL Any humus-rich, well-drained soil
HARDINESS Fully hardy at temperatures down to -15°C/5°F; needs no winter protection
DROUGHT TOLERANCE Excellent, once established
PROBLEMS None
PRUNING Difficult to prune because of its sheer size, so best left to its own devices
PROPAGATION Hardwood cuttings in late autumn

Schizophragma hydrangeoides 'Roseum'
Japanese hydrangea vine

⬆ 12m/40ft ↔ 4m/13ft   **EASY**

A lovely deciduous woody-stemmed climber that requires support in infancy but is effectively self-clinging as it matures. Fairly slow-growing to start with, it has dark green, oval, toothed leaves, and showy, slightly fragrant, creamy white flowers, rather like those of lace-cap hydrangeas. The scent appears to be more potent in the evening. It offers just about everything you would wish for in a climber.

BEST USES Excellent for a north-facing wall, and ideal for growing in containers in shady gardens

FLOWERS July
SCENTED Lightly scented flowers
ASPECT Any, in a sheltered or exposed position; full sun to partial shade
SOIL Any moist, fertile, humus-rich, well-drained soil
HARDINESS Fully hardy at temperatures down to -15°C/5°F; needs no winter protection
DROUGHT TOLERANCE Poor
PROBLEMS None
PRUNING Cut back to maintain size and shape in spring; cut back the flowering shoots to within 2–4 buds of the permanent framework after flowering
PROPAGATION Greenwood or semi-hardwood cuttings in late summer

Clematis

Clematis are a constant source of delight to the gardener, and one of the most enduringly popular groups of climbers. There are more than four hundred species of clematis throughout the world. The majority are fast-growers with relatively small flowers or sepals, but over the last century plant breeders have created many hybrid clematis by crossing one species with another, resulting in clematis of all colours and for all seasons, and with a wide range of flower shapes and sizes. (Interestingly for plants that are much admired for their prolific and colourful flower displays, clematis don't have petals like other flowers, but rather enlarged sepals that form the blooms.)

The most commonly grown varieties are the razzle-dazzle, large-flowered summer hybrids, such as the pale lilac-striped *Clematis* 'Nelly Moser', yet I find these the least appealing of the huge array on offer. They are rather obvious, and you will often see them strangled against a sizzling hot wall, where they shrivel and fade to grey ash in no time. Poor tortured things! Far more interesting are the spring clematis, such as the clear blue-flowered *C.* 'Frances Rivis', the fragrant, creamy white-flowered *C.* 'Apple Blossom' or the flowering pink starburst of *C. montana* var. *rubens* 'Pink Perfection'. The late-summer to autumn flowerers include gems such as the inky purple *C.* 'Royal Velours', the elegant plum-tinted flowers of *C.* 'Vernosa Violacea' or the silvery ghost-like silken seed heads of *C. tangutica*. There are some pretty reliable winter-flowering clematis, too, which can add a touch of floral cheer during those iron-grey winter months. *C. napaulensis*, with its pendent creamy white flowers and drooping pink stamens, is one of my favourites. It is very under-rated, but a real gift in winter.

Clematis 'Bill MacKenzie'

Cultivation

Botanically speaking, clematis are a diverse grouping of plants, but all belong to the large *Ranunculaceae* family. The buttercup is the most well-known member of this group, which may give a hint as to the conditions clematis prefer: heads in the sun and feet in the shade, with their roots kept cool and moist. This is why you will often see pieces of broken flower-pot laid over the soil where a clematis is planted, to help provide this specific require-ment. This also explains why clematis are not drought tolerant: it is recommended that you mulch the base of the plant annually in spring to help prevent water loss from the roots.

The soil should be well drained, as they don't like sitting in waterlogged conditions. Add horticultural grit to heavy clay, to 'open up' the soil and improve the drainage. On sandy soil, dig in some organic matter to bulk up the nutrients and help deliver moisture to the newly planted roots.

Generally, clematis love limey soils, but any reasonably fertile garden soil is suitable.

Although clematis tend to prefer growing in full sun, many will perform adequately in a less desirable location, such as on a north-facing wall that is in shade for much of the day. The flowering will not be so profuse, but as a gardener, needs must, and better some flower in the shade than none at all. Varieties that can cope with a northern aspect include C. 'Nelly Moser', C. *montana* var. *rubens* 'Pink Perfection' and C. 'Elizabeth'.

Some clematis are vigorous enough to cover an entire wall, whilst others have more moderate growth and are much more suitable for container growing. A large clematis grown on a wall will need the support of a framework of garden wires in a grid formation, affixed with vine eyes (see page 95). You may prefer to use trellis instead, but always ensure the trellis is fixed to the wall with wooden battens. This is to allow free circulation of air around the plant as it grows (which will help prevent pests and diseases) and ensures that it is not strangled tightly into the wall. The smaller, more restrained clematis can be grown up obelisks or bamboo supports; twiggy pea sticks or short bamboo canes, interwoven with garden twine, will do the job admirably for herbaceous clematis.

Shallow planting is the main reason gardeners fail with clematis. Plant deeply to ensure that there will always be at least one pair of fresh, healthy buds below the surface level, acting as an emergency fallback if anything untoward happens to the growth above ground. Clematis wilt, which normally affects young plants, and mainly the large-flowered, spring-flowering varieties, could be a problem. Symptoms include shoots wilting (as if the plant has been starved of water) and dying back in isolated areas of the plant. More drastically, the entire plant collapses

and dies. Clematis wilt is a fungal infection, exacerbated by poor drainage, and in the majority of cases seems to strike before the plant blooms. However, the condition is not fully understood, and this deep planting method provides an insurance policy of new buds below soil level if the plant does become infected (see page 104).

Choose a sensible place to dig a planting hole (see page 103). As a general rule of thumb, clematis should be planted some 40cm/15in from a wall and at least 60cm/2ft from the base of a tree or shrub, or they might struggle to establish: the driest garden soil is at the bottom of a wall and clematis roots like water!

It is best not to tie in the young shoots immediately after planting when the clematis is very young, as you may damage the fragile, juvenile stems and make them

The soft, blue flowers of *Clematis* 'Helsingborg' give way to whiskery seed heads after flowering

vulnerable to the clematis wilt fungus. It is enough, initially, to point the plant in the direction you would like it to climb, be patient and in no time at all it will produce sturdier growth that can be gently tied in with a soft garden twine.

In the first two years, take care to ensure that the stems reach their supports easily, without being stretched taut, and that the growth is evenly spaced out so that the plant gets plenty of air circulation and all parts get equal amounts of sun. The large-flowered hybrids respond well to cutting back hard in the first spring after planting, establishing a good 'fan' shape so that the flower display will be open rather than a tangled mess.

There is a tendency to plant clematis and never feed them ever again – see how you'd like it! Feed clematis in spring, either by means of an organic mulch or a liquid feed, but not during their flowering period.

Pruning

People often wonder about the need for pruning clematis at all. In the wild, clematis flower year after year without any pruning, and you may well have a large clematis that flowers beautifully even though you don't prune it. Well, if it ain't broke, don't fix it. Just feed it well and enjoy it.

In some instances pruning is barely necessary except to keep the plant looking tidy and to restrict it within its allocated growing space. C. armandii, C. 'Apple Blossom' and C. cirrhosa var. balearica are all examples of clematis that need minimal pruning. However, the pruning requirements of various clematis differ greatly, and it is as well to understand what to prune and when, as it has a direct impact on the flowering of that particular species. Pruning at the wrong time can greatly reduce the vigour of the plant, lead to complete loss of the flowering display, or even cause the clematis to die. If you're not sure, don't prune. Better to seek advice from the place where you bought the plant or from the British Clematis Society, who will provide very helpful information about all aspects of growing and caring for clematis, or simply wait and observe when it flowers, as the flowering time is often a guide to the pruning time.

Clematis are commonly divided into three categories which indicate how and when they should be pruned (see the chart opposite for a brief explanation). At first glance this appears quite confusing, which has probably put many an aspiring gardener off the whole clematis caper. Don't worry. Once you've got your hand in, you will find it quite simple.

If you are renovating an overgrown clematis that has been neglected for years, follow these simple rules: be as ruthless as you like with the montana varieties, which will rejuvenate with great vigour. Otherwise, proceed with caution. Over, say, a three-year period, prune out a third at a time of any congested masses of tangled, crossed or dead material and always apply a good fertiliser in spring to help the plant recover.

Propagation

Clematis are notoriously difficult to propagate; seed rarely comes true and although rough cuttings 'strike' easily enough, they often die off over the winter. Undoubtedly the most reliable method is layering during the growing season, when the plant is not dormant. The next best option is to take semi-ripe internodal cuttings from mid to late summer, which gives the cuttings a better chance of maturing before the onset of winter.

GROUP 1 *Early-flowering clematis*

These clematis flower in spring on last year's growth of ripened stems. Early-flowering clematis generally produce all their flowers in clusters in May and the flowering tends to be over by the beginning of June.

Clematis belonging to this group (which includes the evergreen, alpina, macropetala and montana species) need no regular pruning: all that is required is a light trim after flowering to maintain size and shape. This is also the ideal time to remove any unwanted stems that may have outgrown their allocated space and cut out any dead wood or weak and straggly-looking stems. Whilst you are about it, it's a good idea to tie in any unruly stems.

GROUP 2 *Early large-flowered hybrid clematis*

The clematis in this group (which includes C. 'Nelly Moser') produce their flowers from May, and some have a second flush of more moderate flowering later in the year. They flower in early summer on the current year's stem growth, which has developed from the previous year's ripened wood.

Light pruning for these clematis is carried out in February or March, at a time when the plant is full of energy and ready to put out new growth. Remove all dead, diseased or weak growth, and cut back to pairs of healthy buds, as these are the buds that will produce this year's flowers.

Thin out any congested stems at the base, aiming for an open, fan-like shape so that the plant is evenly spaced and all parts are receiving much the same amount of sunshine and daylight. Tie the stems firmly to their supports, giving the fresh growth and flowers plenty of air, light and room to develop to their best potential.

GROUP 3 *Late-flowering clematis*

This group includes summer- and autumn-flowering hybrids, such as C. 'M. Koster' (formerly 'Margot Koster') and C. x *durandii*, as well as the viticella and texensis species, and herbaceous varieties. They tend to flower from July onwards and their flowers are produced from the stems grown in the current season.

Prune in mid-February to March before new growth starts. Experience has taught me to wait until March, as a chance frost can damage the emerging buds: a little patience can pay dividends. Cut back hard to a healthy-looking pair of buds, about 15–20cm/6–8in above ground level.

Be brave. This group of clematis responds very well to hard pruning, so sharpen your secateurs and have a go. How far back depends on the state and age of the plant. If it's all a bit bare at the bottom, prune lower, to encourage new growth nearer the base. If you have spent ages training the clematis on an amazing wall or trellis framework, you might quite understandably feel disinclined to prune back that low. As long as you prune down to a healthy pair of buds it doesn't matter how low you go. Just don't cut below an area where you can see no buds.

AUTUMN

Mellow, yellow autumn and the garden is transformed from the gaiety of summer to a more muted palette. Yellows, browns, russets, clarets and tawny golds are the backcloth of the autumn garden, and there are so many wonderful trees, shrubs and bulbs that really come into their own in autumn that a garden without autumn interest is like a sponge cake without icing! There are a great many climbers offering cheerful flowers, vivid foliage, interesting berries and seed heads in this season, helping to prolong the garden's year-long appeal.

Billardiera longiflora
Purple apple berry

⬆ 2m/6ft ⬌ 2m/6ft   MEDIUM

A Tasmanian climbing shrub with narrow, evergreen leaves, mainly grown for its startling purple, metallic berries that are so eye-catching in autumn. It also bears small, heavily scented, creamy green bell-shaped flowers through the summer. In mild areas it can be grown outdoors; otherwise it is best grown in a cool greenhouse or warm conservatory.

BEST USES An unusual climber for the conservatory and ideal for sheltered coastal gardens

FLOWERS June to August, but grown mainly for autumn berries

SCENTED Scented flowers

ASPECT East, south or west facing, in a sheltered position; full sun to partial shade

SOIL Humus-rich, moist, fertile, well-drained soil, preferably loam or sand

HARDINESS Frost hardy at temperatures down to -5°C/23°F; protect roots with a mulch or fleece in winter

DROUGHT TOLERANCE Poor

PROBLEMS Will not tolerate extremes of weather and may suffer leaf loss in very cold conditions

PRUNING Cut out dead and overcrowded growth in spring

PROPAGATION Sow ripe seed in autumn at 13–15°C/55–59°F; semi-ripe cuttings in a propagator in late summer; layering in autumn or spring

GREENFINGER TIP *Benefits from steady protection from winds and shading from full sun*

Clematis flammula
Virgin's bower

⬆ 3.5m/12ft ⬌ 6m/20ft   EASY

This vigorous deciduous climber is grown largely for its sheer abundance of small, vanilla/almond-scented, simple white star-like flowers that last from mid-summer well into autumn. It is literally smothered in them, so you can imagine it is a great lure for pollinating insects. The flowers are followed by silky seed heads in autumn.

BEST USES Grows well through shrubs and small trees, and over tree stumps in dappled shady woodland; also wonderful for growing over spring shrubs that are past their flowering best

FLOWERS August to October
SCENTED Lightly fragrant flowers
ASPECT East, south or west facing, in a sheltered or exposed position; full sun to partial shade
SOIL Any moist, fertile, well-drained soil
HARDINESS Frost hardy at temperatures down to -5°C/23°F; may need winter protection
DROUGHT TOLERANCE Poor
PROBLEMS Clematis wilt
PRUNING In early spring, cut back all the previous year's stems to healthy pairs of buds about 15cm/6in above ground level (Group 3)
PROPAGATION Internodal semi-ripe cuttings in early summer; layering in winter or early spring

Clematis 'Princess Diana' 🎖

⬆ 4m/13ft ⬌ 90cm/3ft   EASY

I first discovered this at an open garden in Long Melford and decided to include it because there are so many Diana devotees out there! Apart from an appealing moniker, it is a dainty, deciduous clematis with very pretty, nodding, tulip-shaped flowers of dark pink that fade as the plant matures. It is very easy to care for and has a long flowering period.

BEST USES A beautiful companion grown through small shrubs, climbing roses and honeysuckles

FLOWERS July to October
SCENTED No
ASPECT East, south or west facing, in a sheltered or exposed position; full sun to partial shade
SOIL Any moist, fertile, well-drained soil
HARDINESS Fully hardy at temperatures down to -15°C/5°F; needs no winter protection
DROUGHT TOLERANCE Poor
PROBLEMS Aphids, caterpillars, earwigs and woolly aphids; clematis wilt
PRUNING In early spring, cut back all the previous year's stems to healthy pairs of buds about 15cm/6in above ground level (Group 3)
PROPAGATION Internodal semi-ripe cuttings in mid to late summer; layering late summer to early autumn

Clematis 'Royal Velours' 🎖

⬆ 3.5m/12ft ↔ 6m/20ft   **EASY**

A vigorous deciduous clematis that produces gorgeous dark purple velvet flowers, with dainty, fine white stamens, in profusion from summer to early autumn. Because this is one of the viticella group of clematis, it has better than average resistance to clematis wilt.

> **BEST USES** Grows well through shrubs and small trees, and over tree stumps; would suit container growing, underplanted with grey-coloured summer bedding foliage plants

FLOWERS August to October
SCENTED No
ASPECT East, south or west facing, in a sheltered or exposed position; full sun to partial shade
SOIL Any moist, fertile, well-drained soil; will thrive in chalky, drier soils
HARDINESS Fully hardy at temperatures down to -15°C/5°F; needs no winter protection
DROUGHT TOLERANCE Poor
PROBLEMS Aphids, caterpillars, earwigs and woolly aphids; clematis wilt
PRUNING In early spring, cut back all the previous year's stems to healthy pairs of buds about 15cm/6in above ground level (Group 3)
PROPAGATION Internodal semi-ripe cuttings in mid to late summer; layering late summer to early autumn

Clematis tibetana subsp. vernayi 'Glasnevin Dusk'

⬆ 2.5m/8ft ↔ 2m/6ft   **EASY**

This is a fairly new clematis, so you might have to search around for it, but I predict a big future for 'Glasnevin Dusk'. It has rather unusual grey-green foliage in contrast to the more typical green leaves of other varieties of clematis, and the most gorgeous, dusky damson-coloured flowers, about 5cm/2in across, that resemble small hanging sea urchins, until the sepals peel back to reveal golden stamens. It flowers for a very long period.

> **BEST USES** Great at the back of borders and an easy subject in patio containers as it reaches a restrained height; also excellent for roof terraces

FLOWERS June to October
SCENTED No
ASPECT East, south or west facing, in a sheltered or exposed position; full sun to partial shade
SOIL Any moist, fertile, well-drained soil
HARDINESS Fully hardy at temperatures down to -15°C/5°F; needs no winter protection
DROUGHT TOLERANCE Poor
PROBLEMS Clematis wilt
PRUNING In early spring, cut back all the previous year's stems to healthy pairs of buds about 15cm/6in above ground level (Group 3)
PROPAGATION Internodal semi-ripe cuttings in mid to late summer; layering late summer to early autumn

Cobaea scandens ☻
Cup and saucer vine

⬆ 3m/10ft ⬌ 90cm/3ft EASY

Originally from the South American tropics, this climbing vine is nothing short of delightful. Usually grown as an annual in colder climes, it has large, scented, cup-shaped flowers of creamy green and purple from summer to the first frosts. A great favourite of Vita Sackville-West, so if it's good enough for her, it's good enough for us! *Cobea scandens* f. *alba* ☻ is a pretty white variety that is well worth trying.

BEST USES Grow as an annual on south- or west-facing walls or up bamboo tepees in containers and then plunge in bare spaces in the border

FLOWERS August to November
SCENTED Scented flowers
ASPECT South, east or west facing, in a sheltered position; full sun
SOIL Any moist, fertile, well-drained soil, particularly loam and sand
HARDINESS Frost tender, not hardy at temperatures below 5°C/41°F; grow as an annual in all but the mildest areas, or overwinter in a greenhouse and move outside in summer
DROUGHT TOLERANCE Poor
PROBLEMS Red spider mite, when grown under glass
PRUNING None; it will die back naturally with the first frosts
PROPAGATION Sow seed in spring at 18C°/64°F

Cotoneaster horizontalis ☻
Wall spray

⬆ 90cm/3ft ⬌ 1.5m/5ft EASY

A small deciduous shrub easily trained as a wall climber. It has small, round, dark green glossy leaves that mature to red orange in autumn, and bright red autumn berries. Though grown mainly for its berry display, it bears pretty, small, pinkish flowers in spring. The flat, fish-boned formation of the branches looks very eye-catching even in deepest winter.

BEST USES An incredibly versatile, attractive, neat shrub, ideal for growing around porches and doorways or against low walls

FLOWERS May, but grown mainly for berries
SCENTED No
ASPECT East, south or west facing, in an exposed or sheltered position; full sun to partial shade
SOIL Any fertile, well-drained soil
HARDINESS Fully hardy at temperatures down to -15°C/5°F; needs no winter protection
DROUGHT TOLERANCE Excellent, once established
PROBLEMS Aphids; fireblight
PRUNING Minimal; trim in late winter or early spring, removing dead, damaged or crossed stems
PROPAGATION Sow fresh seed in autumn (does not come reliably true); layering in spring; greenwood cuttings in early summer

GREENFINGER TIP *This shrub's many attributes are often overlooked as it is so common. However, it is one of the rare shrubs that looks good all year round*

Pyracantha rogersiana ♒
Asian firethorn

⬆ 4m/13ft ⬌ 4m/13ft　　　　　EASY

This evergreen shrub has glossy green leaves, with small, pretty, white flowers in early summer, followed by a profusion of red to orange berries in autumn. The thorns are vicious, but it is low maintenance and very drought tolerant once established.

BEST USES Planted against a low wall or as a hedge, the thorns help deter roaming pets or other pests such as rabbits and deer; also very handsome planted to frame doorways or garden gates

FLOWERS June, but grown mainly for evergreen foliage and autumn berries

SCENTED No

ASPECT East, south or west facing, in a sheltered or exposed position; full sun to partial shade

SOIL Any moist, fertile, well-drained soil

HARDINESS Fully hardy at temperatures down to -15°C/5°F; needs no winter protection

DROUGHT TOLERANCE Excellent, once established

PROBLEMS Aphids, caterpillars and woolly aphids; fireblight

PRUNING Cut back any stems growing out of line to keep it to its allocated space, and prune out old berry clusters in spring, to make room for new growth

PROPAGATION Semi-ripe cuttings in late summer to autumn

Pyracantha Saphyr Orange
(also known as 'Cadange') Firethorn

⬆ 4m/13ft ⬌ 3m/10ft　　　　　EASY

Although usually grown as a hedge, firethorn can also be grown as a wall climber. It is evergreen with thorny branches and small white flowers that appear in late spring, but is mainly grown for its prolific red-orange berries, which are produced in autumn. Once established, it is very drought tolerant. Watch those thorns!

BEST USES Provides very effective colour for the autumn garden, particularly when planted with red-stemmed dogwood; can be trained to fill arches or doorways, and birds like to eat the berries; very tolerant of pollution, so ideal for city areas

FLOWERS May, but grown mainly for evergreen foliage and autumn berries

SCENTED No

ASPECT East, south or west facing, in a sheltered or exposed position; full sun to partial shade

SOIL Any moist, fertile, well-drained soil

HARDINESS Fully hardy at temperatures down to -15°C/5°F; needs no winter protection

DROUGHT TOLERANCE Excellent, once established

PROBLEMS Aphids, caterpillars and woolly aphids; fireblight

PRUNING Cut back straggling stems in spring, and trim lightly to restrict size and shape

PROPAGATION Semi-ripe cuttings in late summer to autumn

Rosa 'Zéphirine Drouhin'

⬆ 3m/10ft ⬌ 3m/10ft   EASY

This climbing rose has become popular because it will flower on a north wall and is almost thornless, but it is very prone to mildew. That said, it has attractive large, loose, deeply fragrant rose pink flowers in summer. These are borne quite freely, and modestly repeat again in early autumn.

BEST USES Will flower reliably on a north-facing wall and looks good growing up a trellis, over a pergola or along a wooden or picket fence; I first saw it as an informal hedge, which looked beautiful in full flower, and still prefer to see it this way

FLOWERS June to September
SCENTED Scented flowers
ASPECT Any, in a sheltered position; full sun to partial shade
SOIL Any fertile, well-drained soil
HARDINESS Fully hardy at temperatures down to -15°C/5°F; needs no winter protection
DROUGHT TOLERANCE Excellent, once established
PROBLEMS Aphids, caterpillars and scale insect; fairly disease resistant
PRUNING Deadhead regularly, cut out damaged stems in late autumn to early spring, and reduce a third of the oldest remaining shoots to just above soil level; if growing as a hedge, trim lightly with a hedgecutter
PROPAGATION Hardwood cuttings in late autumn

Sollya heterophylla ♟
Bluebell creeper

⬆ 2m/6ft ⬌ 60cm/2ft   MEDIUM

An elegant and restrained evergreen climber with narrow, dark green leaves and clusters of charming bright blue flowers produced in summer to autumn. It has pretty inky blue berries after flowering which are attractive to wildlife. In terms of year-round interest, it has much to recommend it.

BEST USES A slightly unusual climber for small courtyards, borders and containers, combining well with any yellow-leaved shrubs and plants

FLOWERS June to September, but also grown for evergreen foliage and autumn berries
SCENTED No
ASPECT East, south or west facing, in a sheltered position; full sun to partial shade
SOIL Any humus-rich, fertile, well-drained soil
HARDINESS Half hardy at temperatures down to 0°C/32°F; needs protection from frosts
DROUGHT TOLERANCE Poor
PROBLEMS Red spider mite when grown under glass
PRUNING Minimal; shorten side shoots to three buds in late winter or early spring
PROPAGATION Sow seed in spring at 10–16°C/50–61°F; softwood cuttings in late spring or winter

GREENFINGER TIP *As winters become milder, try growing sollya outdoors: it survives well with protection*

Thunbergia alata
Black-eyed Susan

⬆ 2.5m/8ft ⬌ 60cm/2ft   **EASY**

A cheery, cheeky, fast-growing annual climber with light green, oval to heart-shaped leaves. The flowers are a lively yellow-orange with dark brown eyes, and are borne in abundance from early summer to autumn; the leaves display the bold colour very well indeed.

BEST USES Looks great in hanging baskets, but also useful to bring a splash of hot colour to exotic borders, and will do very well in containers

FLOWERS July to October

SCENTED No

ASPECT South or west facing, in a sheltered position; full sun

SOIL Any fertile, well-drained soil

HARDINESS Frost tender, not hardy at temperatures below 5°C/41°F; usually grown as an annual

DROUGHT TOLERANCE Poor

PROBLEMS None

PRUNING None, as will die back with the first frosts

PROPAGATION Sow seed in spring at 16–18°C/ 61–64°F

GREENFINGER TIP *This is easily raised from seed and is so trouble free and profuse in flowering that it's really worth trying to find a spot for it somewhere*

Tropaeolum speciosum 🏅
Flame creeper/Scot's flame flower

⬆ 3m/10ft ⬌ 90cm/3ft   **MEDIUM**

Originating from Central/South America, this slender, climbing herbaceous perennial has mid-green rounded leaves, forming a palm-shaped grouping. From mid-summer to autumn it is literally smothered in vivid, bright red-coloured flowers, very like nasturtiums in appearance, but then it is from the same family. It has tuberous roots.

BEST USES Grown through an evergreen tree or shrub, it adds exotic interest to sombre hedging and trees, and is particularly effective with yew; will even give the much loathed *leylandii* a run for its money

FLOWERS June to October

SCENTED No

ASPECT East, south or west facing, in a sheltered position; full sun to partial shade

SOIL Rich, deep, moisture-retentive soil is best; adding leaf mould will help to establish the plant

HARDINESS Frost hardy at temperatures down to -5°C/23°F; tubers can be buried deeply in mild areas or lifted before the first frosts in harsher regions

DROUGHT TOLERANCE Poor

PROBLEMS Cabbage butterflies; can be hard to establish if the tubers have been allowed to dry out

PRUNING None, as will die back with the first frosts

PROPAGATION Division in early spring; stem-tip cuttings with bottom heat in late summer

Celastrus scandens
American bittersweet/Staff tree

⬆ 7m/22ft ↔ 2m/6ft   **EASY**

This deciduous twining climber is grown largely for its autumn interest. It has mid-green leaves which turn to yellow in autumn, and tiny upright stems of small, insignificant white flowers in summer. It is the exuberant clusters of golden and scarlet berries that really command attention.

BEST USES Grow over tree stumps and through shrubs and trees to prolong seasonal interest; the autumn colour also looks super against soft red brick or old stone walls; ideal for the cottage or wildlife garden as birds and animals love the berries

FLOWERS July to August, but grown mainly for autumn foliage and berries

SCENTED No

ASPECT Any, in a sheltered or exposed position; full sun to partial shade

SOIL Any moist, fertile, well-drained soil

HARDINESS Fully hardy at temperatures down to -15°C/5°F; needs no winter protection

DROUGHT TOLERANCE Poor

PROBLEMS None

PRUNING Cut out any dead, diseased or damaged material in late winter or early spring to maintain size and shape; shorten and tie in young stems in March

PROPAGATION Greenwood or softwood cuttings in early summer; root cuttings in winter

GREENFINGER TIP *Male and female flowers are on separate plants, and for good berry displays you will need to plant both varieties: ask the advice of your local nursery*

Clematis 'Bill MacKenzie' 🎖

⬆ 8m/26ft ↔ 4m/13ft   **EASY**

An energetic autumn-flowering clematis with small, golden yellow, hanging bell-shaped flowers that have four distinct sepals, rather like a peeled fruit. The dainty flowers are followed by very attractive large, ornamental, silky seed heads. This will tolerate shady, north-facing walls.

BEST USES Ideal for growing in smaller shady city gardens because of its tolerance of north-facing aspects, and will do well in containers; fabulous for lively autumn colour and striking seed heads

FLOWERS September to October

SCENTED No

ASPECT Any, in a sheltered or exposed position; full sun to partial shade

SOIL Any moist, fertile, humus-rich, well-drained soil

HARDINESS Fully hardy at temperatures down to -15°C/5°F; needs no winter protection

DROUGHT TOLERANCE Poor

PROBLEMS Aphids, caterpillars and earwigs; clematis wilt

PRUNING In early spring, before the emergence of new growth, cut back all the previous year's stems to healthy pairs of buds about 15cm/6in above ground level (Group 3)

PROPAGATION Internodal semi-ripe cuttings in mid to late summer; layering late summer to early autumn

Clematis tangutica

⬆ 6m/20ft ⬌ 3m/10ft   EASY

A lovely autumn-flowering clematis that is fairly fast-growing. In late summer to autumn it is smothered in an abundance of nodding, yellow bell-shaped flowers with an orange-peel effect, followed by fluffy seed heads which remain prettily on the plant for several weeks.

BEST USES Ideal for growing against a wall behind flower borders and over sheds, old brick buildings and fences; lovely in the cottage garden

FLOWERS September to October

SCENTED No

ASPECT East, south or west facing, in a sheltered or exposed position; full sun to partial shade

SOIL Any moist, fertile, humus-rich, well-drained soil

HARDINESS Fully hardy at temperatures down to -15°C/5°F; needs no winter protection

DROUGHT TOLERANCE Poor

PROBLEMS Aphids, caterpillars and earwigs; clematis wilt

PRUNING In early spring, before the emergence of new growth, cut back all the previous year's stems to healthy pairs of buds about 15cm/6in above ground level; for best effect, allow the plant to spread sideways and tie in to supports (Group 3)

PROPAGATION Internodal semi-ripe cuttings in mid to late summer; layering late summer to early autumn

Cotoneaster frigidus 'Cornubia' ♊
Tree cotoneaster

⬆ 8m/26ft ⬌ 8m/26ft   EASY

A mainly evergreen, fast-growing shrub, ideal as a wall climber, with clusters of white summer flowers and small, round, shiny dark green leaves, bronze as they mature. Clusters of bright red berries are borne in autumn. Common though it may be, it is one of those reliable plants that works for you 365 days a year, without demanding too much of your time.

BEST USES Ideal as a small wall climber on a shady wall where the berries will liven up the winter garden, and in the wildlife garden, as birds also love the berries

FLOWERS June, but grown mainly for autumn berries

SCENTED No

ASPECT Any, in a sheltered or exposed position; full sun to partial shade

SOIL Any fertile, well-drained soil

HARDINESS Fully hardy at temperatures down to -15°C/5°F; needs no winter protection

DROUGHT TOLERANCE Good, once established

PROBLEMS Fireblight

PRUNING Remove any unsightly or damaged stems after flowering, to maintain shape and size

PROPAGATION Greenwood or softwood cuttings from spring to mid-summer; semi-ripe cuttings in late summer; layering in spring

Lonicera x italica ♀
Italian honeysuckle

⬆ 8m/26ft ⬌ 60cm/2ft   **EASY**

A gorgeous, fast-growing and particularly fragrant honeysuckle with mid-green oval leaves and masses of sweetly fragrant, white, trumpet-shaped flowers that turn to yellow and are flushed purple in the summer months. It has clusters of vivid red berries in autumn.

BEST USES An informal climber for the cottage garden that is ideal left to climb over pergolas, old outbuildings, sheds or trained along long runs of fencing, and charming as an informal hedge; a real draw for wildlife, pollinating bees being attracted to the flowers and birds to the berries; tolerant of coastal conditions

FLOWERS July to October, with autumn berry display

SCENTED Highly scented flowers

ASPECT Any, in a sheltered or exposed position; full sun to full shade

SOIL Any moist, fertile, humus-rich, well-drained soil

HARDINESS Fully hardy at temperatures down to -15°C/5°F; needs no winter protection

DROUGHT TOLERANCE Good, once established

PROBLEMS None

PRUNING Cut back mature plants after flowering by removing a third of the flowering shoots each year

PROPAGATION Softwood or semi-ripe cuttings in spring to late summer; hardwood cuttings in late autumn to mid-winter; layering in spring

Lonicera periclymenum 'Serotina' ♀
Late Dutch honeysuckle

⬆ 8m/26ft ⬌ 90cm/3ft   **EASY**

This is a much-loved honeysuckle, long a traditional cottage garden favourite. It's a value-for-money climber with a long flowering period and heavenly scented creamy white flowers streaked with purple red. Small red berries are produced in autumn.

BEST USES An informal climber that is easy to grow over almost any garden structure or boundary; useful for livening up a shady north wall, and tolerant of coastal conditions

FLOWERS July to October, with autumn berry display

SCENTED Scented flowers

ASPECT Any, in a sheltered or exposed position; full sun to partial shade

SOIL Any moist, fertile, humus-rich, well-drained soil

HARDINESS Fully hardy at temperatures down to -15°C/5°F; needs no winter protection

DROUGHT TOLERANCE Good, once established

PROBLEMS None

PRUNING Cut back each year after flowering to young, healthy shoots

PROPAGATION Softwood or semi-ripe cuttings in spring to late summer; hardwood cuttings in late autumn to mid-winter; layering in spring

Solanum crispum
Potato vine

⬆ 6m/20ft ⬌ 6m/20ft   EASY

A fast-growing evergreen climber with a scrambling habit, producing clusters of lightly fragrant, dainty pale mauve flowers with yellow eyes. It flowers in summer, but continues flowering until the first frosts in late autumn, when there is a dearth of flowering climbers. It has attractive, small, lance-shaped green leaves, with tiny, pale yellow berries after flowering, and is very easy to grow. *S. crispum* 'Glasnevin' ♈ is an appealing, more compact and free-flowering variety that is also worth considering.

BEST USES Perfect on a sheltered, warm, sunny wall, providing a lengthy flowering period

FLOWERS July to November
SCENTED Slightly scented flowers
ASPECT Any, in a sheltered position; full sun
SOIL Any fertile, well-drained soil
HARDINESS Frost hardy at temperatures down to -5°C/23°F; may need winter protection in cold regions
DROUGHT TOLERANCE Good, once established
PROBLEMS None
PRUNING Cut back to three or four buds of the original framework in late winter or early spring
PROPAGATION Sow seed in late winter to early spring; softwood or semi-ripe cuttings in late spring to late summer

GREENFINGER TIP *It needs plenty of support from first planting as it has a very rapid growth rate and the leaf mass can get fairly weighty*

Solanum laxum 'Album' ♈
(formerly *S. jasminoides* 'Album')

⬆ 6m/20ft ⬌ 6m/20ft   EASY

A fast-growing, evergreen scrambling climber that flowers from summer to the first frosts, offering a very long season of flowering interest. It bears a profusion of small, barely scented but pretty clusters of pure white flowers with cheery yellow middles. Tiny black berries are produced after flowering. It needs plenty of support from first planting as it has such a rapid growth rate.

BEST USES Useful on a sheltered, warm, sunny wall, providing a lengthy flowering period, with the bonus of berries in autumn; this has much the same growing habit as *Solanum crispum*, so it really comes down to which flower colour you prefer

FLOWERS July to November
SCENTED Slightly scented flowers
ASPECT South or west facing, in a sheltered position; full sun
SOIL Any moist, fertile, well-drained soil
HARDINESS Frost hardy at temperatures down to -5°C/23°F; may need winter protection in cold regions
DROUGHT TOLERANCE Good, once established
PROBLEMS None
PRUNING Cut back to three or four buds of the original framework in late winter
PROPAGATION Sow seed in late winter to early spring; softwood or semi-ripe cuttings in late spring to late summer

Vitis vinifera 'Purpurea' ♉
Tenturier or Dyer's grape

⬆ 6m/20ft ⬌ 5.5m/18ft   **EASY**

A most attractive, deciduous, fast-growing, tendrilled vine grown mainly for its grey-green foliage that turns a muted plummy claret in autumn. It produces dark purple grapes; these are bitter, but the birds love them and they look very ornamental against the leaves. It will need strong support from the outset, as the leaf mass gets fairly weighty.

BEST USES Leave to scramble wildly through a dull tree or to brighten a long stretch of wall or brick work; the summer foliage is very attractive over an outside dining area, providing light dappled shade

FLOWERS May to June, but grown mainly for autumn foliage

SCENTED No

ASPECT South or west facing, in a sheltered position; full sun to partial shade

SOIL Any fertile, humus-enriched, well-drained soil

HARDINESS Fully hardy at temperatures down to -15°C/5°F; needs no winter protection

DROUGHT TOLERANCE Good, once established

PROBLEMS Powdery mildew

PRUNING In January, cut back the side shoots from the main stems, leaving about two buds

PROPAGATION Sow seed or layer in spring; softwood or semi-ripe cuttings from late spring to mid-summer; hardwood cuttings in late autumn or winter

Campsis radicans f. *flava* ♉
Yellow trumpet creeper/Yellow trumpet vine

⬆ 10m/32ft ⬌ 5m/16ft   **EASY**

An energetic deciduous climber that clings by aerial roots. It has absolutely spectacular clusters of clear yellow tubular flowers that are attractive to pollinating insects, with dark green toothed foliage. Ornamental winged seed pods follow after flowering. It needs to be supported on a framework of wires for the first two or three years, but is self-clinging once it matures.

BEST USES Perfect for bringing an exotic touch to the garden and very suitable for the Mediterranean garden; ideal for climbing up a warm, sunny wall or pillar

FLOWERS August to September

SCENTED No

ASPECT South or west facing, in a sheltered or exposed position; full sun

SOIL Any fertile, well-drained soil

HARDINESS Fully hardy at temperatures down to -15°C/5°F; needs no winter protection

DROUGHT TOLERANCE Poor

PROBLEMS None

PRUNING Once established, it should be cut back in early winter to control shape and spread by removing any old, straggling, crossed or damaged stems

PROPAGATION Sow seed in spring; semi-ripe cuttings in summer; hardwood cuttings from autumn to mid-winter; root cuttings in winter; layering in winter

Celastrus orbiculatus
Oriental bittersweet

⬆ 14m/46ft ⬌ 8m/26ft   EASY

This twining climbing shrub is grown mainly for autumn interest, when its round, often scalloped, bright green leaves turn mellow yellow and it produces generous clusters of golden berries, which split to reveal scarlet seeds and last for some months, if the birds don't get there first! In early summer it has rather ordinary, plain white to green flowers. It needs early support, but the stems are fairly self-clinging, so it seldom needs much tying in.

BEST USES Particularly useful for training up large trees and fences, where the fruits will be exposed to the sun that they need to achieve their best colour; the extended berry display is a great lure for wildlife

FLOWERS June to July, but grown mainly for autumn foliage and berries

SCENTED No

ASPECT East, south or west facing, in a sheltered or exposed position; full sun to partial shade

SOIL Any fertile, well-drained soil

HARDINESS Fully hardy at temperatures down to -15°C/5°F; needs no winter protection

DROUGHT TOLERANCE Poor

PROBLEMS None

PRUNING Cut back in late winter and early spring to maintain size and shape

PROPAGATION Greenwood or softwood cuttings in summer; root cuttings in winter

Parthenocissus henryana 🎖
Chinese Virginia creeper

⬆ 10m/32ft ⬌ 5m/16ft   EASY

The self-clinging, large, mid-green leaves of this deciduous vine are deeply divided with really pronounced creamy veins and attractive pink flushing at the leaf base. In autumn the leaves are burnished crimson in colour, and the veining turns silver. It has plain, pale green flowers, and blackish berries are sometimes produced after hot summers. This will need strong supports from infancy, but the leaf display is phenomenal.

BEST USES Slightly more restrained than other vines, so ideal for a modest garden, but also looks awesome clothing a large brick wall

FLOWERS June to August, but grown mainly for autumn foliage

SCENTED No

ASPECT Any, in a sheltered or exposed position; full sun to full shade

SOIL Any fertile, well-drained soil

HARDINESS Fully hardy at temperatures down to -15°C/5°F; needs no winter protection

DROUGHT TOLERANCE Good, once established

PROBLEMS Red spider mite and vine weevil

PRUNING Cut back in mid-winter to maintain size and spread; keep well away from guttering and windows

PROPAGATION Softwood cuttings in early summer; greenwood cuttings in mid-summer; hardwood cuttings in winter; layering in spring

Parthenocissus quinquefolia ℘
Virginia creeper

⬆ 15m/50ft ⬌ 5m/16ft   EASY

A handsome, deciduous self-clinging climber that has spectacular autumn colour, is easy to grow and very vigorous, so you will need to give it a lot of space. A large north- or east-facing wall, where you can really appreciate the brilliant fiery reds of its autumn foliage and its modest crop of blue-black fruits, is the perfect canvas. It has insignificant greenish flowers in summer.

BEST USES Dazzling for covering an ugly house or shady, north-facing garage walls; also fairly salt tolerant, so will do well for coastal gardeners

FLOWERS June to August, but grown mainly for autumn foliage

SCENTED No

ASPECT Any, in a sheltered or exposed position; full sun to full shade

SOIL Any fertile, well-drained soil

HARDINESS Fully hardy at temperatures down to -15°C/5°F; needs no winter protection

DROUGHT TOLERANCE Good, once established

PROBLEMS Red spider mite and vine weevil

PRUNING Once established, cut back in early winter to keep the plant stems from intruding into windows, guttering and roofs

PROPAGATION Softwood cuttings in early summer; greenwood cuttings in mid-summer; hardwood cuttings in winter; layering in spring

GREENFINGER TIP *Planting this climber in a sunny position results in much stronger colour variation*

Parthenocissus tricuspidata 'Veitchii'
Japanese ivy 'Veitchii'

⬆ 20m/65ft ⬌ 10m/32ft   EASY

A sunny autumn day really shows this elegant climber at its best. The handsome, deeply lobed, glossy dark green leaves turn spectacular shades of red and purple in autumn and the results are even more dramatic if it is planted in a sunny position. It bears insignificant greenish flowers and sometimes, after long hot summers, black berries are produced. It will need sturdy support in its first two years, but is self-clinging once established.

BEST USES Superb for a large north- or east-facing wall; mature plants provide a wonderful habitat for birds

FLOWERS June to August, but grown mainly for autumn foliage

SCENTED No

ASPECT Any, in a sheltered or exposed position; full sun to full shade

SOIL Any fertile, well-drained soil

HARDINESS Fully hardy at temperatures down to -15°C/5°F; needs no winter protection

DROUGHT TOLERANCE Good, once established

PROBLEMS Leaf spot and vine weevil

PRUNING Needs cutting back regularly in early winter to keep it under control and prevent it climbing onto roofs and gutters

PROPAGATION Softwood cuttings in early summer; greenwood cuttings in mid-summer; hardwood cuttings in winter; layering in spring

Pileostegia viburnoides ♈

⬆ 10m/32ft ↔ 4m/13ft   EASY

This is a slow-growing, low-maintenance, evergreen climber that will need early support but is reasonably self-clinging as it matures. It has long, dark green leathery leaves and bears numerous large panicles of slightly fragrant, off-white star-shaped flowers from late summer into autumn. It used to be quite difficult to buy, but I am assured many nurseries now stock it.

BEST USES Very striking for growing up smaller shrubs and trees: because of its moderate growth rate, it will never swamp its host

FLOWERS July to October, but also grown for evergreen foliage

SCENTED Lightly scented flowers

ASPECT Any, in a sheltered or exposed position; full sun to partial shade

SOIL Any moist, fertile, well-drained soil

HARDINESS Frost hardy at temperatures down to -5°C/23°F; may need winter protection

DROUGHT TOLERANCE Poor

PROBLEMS None, but it can be slow to establish

PRUNING Minimal

PROPAGATION Semi-ripe cuttings in summer; layering in spring

Vitis amurensis
Amur grape

⬆ 15m/50ft ↔ 6m/20ft   EASY

An unusual, tendrilled deciduous vine, which is an excellent foliage plant with striking, large green leaves, up to 25cm/10in across, that change to vivid crimson, purple and gold in autumn. It has small green flowers and bears edible, slightly bitter grapes in autumn. It is vigorous, so you will need considerable space to grow it.

BEST USES Grow on strong supports over an outdoor dining area where the splendid leaves will cast attractive shade; looks absolutely stunning left to its own devices, climbing up large, evergreen trees

FLOWERS May to July, but grown mainly for autumn foliage

SCENTED No

ASPECT South or west facing, in a sheltered position; full sun to partial shade

SOIL Any fertile, humus-enriched, well-drained soil

HARDINESS Fully hardy at temperatures down to -15°C/5°F; needs no winter protection

DROUGHT TOLERANCE Poor

PROBLEMS Powdery mildew

PRUNING Prune in winter when the plant is dormant, to restrict size and shape

PROPAGATION Sow seed or layer in spring; softwood or semi-ripe cuttings from late spring to mid-summer; hardwood cuttings in late autumn or winter

Vitis coignetiae 🎖
Crimson glory vine

⬆ 15m/50ft ↔ 5m/16ft   **EASY**

This extremely vigorous deciduous vine has striking, dark green heart-shaped leaves with distinct veining and lightly scented, small green flowers. It produces rather small, unpalatable grapes. The undersides of the leaf are felty brown and turn a brilliant wine-red in autumn, making a spectacular sight with the late autumn sun slanting through them. This will need strong support from the start.

BEST USES Leave to scramble through a large, dull tree; will cover large unsightly walls in no time

FLOWERS May to June, but grown mainly for autumn foliage

SCENTED Lightly scented flowers

ASPECT South or west facing, in a sheltered position; full sun

SOIL Any fertile, humus-enriched, well-drained soil

HARDINESS Fully hardy to -15°C/5°F, but late frosts can cause extensive leaf damage (the plant will recover)

DROUGHT TOLERANCE Poor

PROBLEMS Powdery mildew

PRUNING Cut back to three or four buds from the main stem framework in February, when dormant; shorten young shoots again, more lightly, in summer to restrict it to its allocated space; if grown up a tree, its size will make pruning impossible

PROPAGATION Sow seed or layer in spring; softwood or semi-ripe cuttings from late spring to mid-summer; hardwood cuttings in late autumn or winter

Vitis vinifera 'Siegerrebe'

⬆ 15m/50ft ↔ 3.5m/12ft   **MEDIUM**

A vigorous deciduous vine with large green leaves that age to purple and deep red in autumn. Delicious, sweet-tasting white dessert grapes are produced in late summer to early autumn, but the crop can be meagre. This vine can potentially grow very large, so it will require strong supports and regular tying in of stems from the very start.

BEST USES Ideal trained along walls and fences in a kitchen garden or at the back of a long border; excellent for a large pergola

FLOWERS June to July, but grown mainly for autumn foliage

SCENTED No

ASPECT South or west facing, in a sheltered position; full sun

SOIL Any fertile, humus-enriched, well-drained soil

HARDINESS Fully hardy at temperatures down to -15°C/5°F; needs no winter protection

DROUGHT TOLERANCE Poor

PROBLEMS Mealybug and red spider mite; powdery mildew

PRUNING Cut back in mid-winter when the plant is dormant, to restrict its rampant inclinations

PROPAGATION Sow seed or layer in spring; softwood or semi-ripe cuttings from late spring to mid-summer; hardwood cuttings in late autumn or winter

GREENFINGER TIP *The grape crop is relatively small and early, and you should pick them as they ripen or the birds will beat you to it!*

WINTER

Winter doesn't have to be a cheerless time in the garden; there are many plants that really come into their own as the weather turns cold and the dark nights draw in. Just as you are settling yourself into hibernation mode, some truly lovely garden plants are readying themselves to take centre stage in the garden, without any of the accustomed rivalry from their later-flowering neighbours. Think about adding evergreen foliage, winter-flowering climbers or livid-berried shrubs to the winter garden, bringing life and colour to a fading landscape that transforms your garden into a place of wonder 365 days a year.

Chimonanthus praecox 'Luteus' 🎖
Wintersweet

⬆ 4m/13ft ↔ 4m/13ft　　　　　EASY

This deciduous, fairly bushy shrub can be coaxed from free-standing shrub to wall climber by tying in the stems horizontally to a framework of wires as it develops. It is worth growing for the sweetly fragrant, cupped, lemon-yellow pendent flowers, borne charmingly on bare winter stems. The flowers are slightly stained with rusty purple inside and are a great boost to winter floral arrangements.

BEST USES A useful shrub grown by the back door or under a window to appreciate the light spicy winter scent

FLOWERS December to February
SCENTED Lightly scented flowers
ASPECT South or west facing, in a sheltered position; full sun
SOIL Any fertile, well-drained soil
HARDINESS Fully hardy at temperatures down to -15°C/5°F; in severe winters young wood may be damaged by frosts
DROUGHT TOLERANCE Poor
PROBLEMS None
PRUNING Minimal; cut back after flowering to maintain size and shape, removing any dead or damaged material
PROPAGATION Heeled softwood cuttings in summer; layering in autumn

Clematis cirrhosa var. *balearica*
Balearic clematis

⬆ 3m/10ft ⬌ 1.5m/5ft   EASY

Don't be deceived by this dainty, tendrilled, evergreen clematis, originally from the Balearics: it's tougher than it looks. In winter it has lightly fragrant, creamy white, bell-shaped flowers, speckled inside with rust maroon flecking, and delicate bronze-tinted evergreen leaves.

BEST USES Excellent climber for growing in containers as it is of infinitely manageable proportions; site near a door or window where the delicate perfume can really be appreciated on a winter's day

FLOWERS January to February
SCENTED Lightly scented flowers
ASPECT South or west facing, in a sheltered position; full sun to partial shade
SOIL Any fertile, well-drained soil
HARDINESS Frost hardy at temperatures down to -5°C/23°F; may not survive severe winters, but protection should see it through in most areas
DROUGHT TOLERANCE Poor
PROBLEMS Clematis wilt
PRUNING Minimal; if space is restricted, give it a light trim after flowering, and remove dead or damaged material (Group 1)
PROPAGATION Internodal semi-ripe cuttings in mid to late summer; layering late summer to early autumn

Clematis cirrhosa var. *purpurascens* 'Freckles' ♗

⬆ 4m/13ft ⬌ 90cm/3ft   EASY

A delightful winter clematis that really earns its keep when not much else is in flower. It is similar in appearance to *C. cirrhosa* var. *balearica*, with a profusion of fragrant, freckled, plummy purple flowers with white margins, followed by silken seed heads. The dainty evergreen foliage looks pretty and tidy nearly all year round, and its tendrils make it fairly self-supporting, though the main stems may need tying in.

BEST USES A useful, attractive, but moderately growing clematis for a small, sunny courtyard garden or tiny rear patio, offering all-season interest

FLOWERS November to February
SCENTED Lightly scented flowers
ASPECT South or west facing, in a sheltered position; full sun
SOIL Any fertile, well-drained soil
HARDINESS Frost hardy at temperatures down to -5°C/23°F; may not survive severe winters, but protection should see it through in most areas
DROUGHT TOLERANCE Poor
PROBLEMS Caterpillars and earwigs; clematis wilt
PRUNING Minimal; trim after flowering, and remove dead or damaged growth when necessary (Group 1)
PROPAGATION Internodal semi-ripe cuttings in mid to late summer; layering late summer to early autumn

Cotoneaster lacteus 🏅
Late cotoneaster

⬆ 4m/13ft ⬌ 4m/13ft   EASY

An attractive evergreen shrub with rather lax
stems, so it is easily trained as a hedge or formal
climber by tying in the stems to a strong
framework of garden wires. It has dark green
leaves with distinct veining, and pendulous
clusters of bright red fruits from autumn to
winter. The white flowers in summer are a bonus.

BEST USES Perfect for covering banks and slopes
or as handsome formal hedging along a low wall
or concrete-posted fence; will also do well in
containers in a city garden or on a roof terrace

FLOWERS June to July, but grown mainly for evergreen
foliage and berry display

SCENTED No

ASPECT Any, in a sheltered or exposed position; full sun
to full shade

SOIL Any fertile, well-drained soil

HARDINESS Fully hardy at temperatures down to
-15°C/5°F; needs no winter protection

DROUGHT TOLERANCE Excellent, once established

PROBLEMS Vine weevil; fireblight and powdery mildew

PRUNING Minimal; prune for shape and size after the
berries have formed, and remove dead or damaged
growth

PROPAGATION Semi-ripe cuttings late summer;
layering in spring

....

GREENFINGER TIP *This is a useful plant for seaside
gardens as it is tolerant of coastal conditions, including
exposure to salt-laden winds; it is also tolerant of pollution*

Euonymus fortunei 'Emerald 'n' Gold' 🏅

⬆ 50cm/20in ⬌ 90cm/3ft   EASY

This evergreen dwarf shrub has bright green
leaves with gold edging, slightly flushed with
pink in winter. A negligible crop of ordinary,
greenish flowers are occasionally produced. It
can easily be encouraged as a wall climber, and
will naturally lean up against any wall.

BEST USES A neat, modest shrub that is the ideal
low-maintenance climber for smaller spaces or tiny
shaded gardens; often grown around doorways or
even as a low-growing hedge

FLOWERS Insignificant or absent; grown for foliage

SCENTED No

ASPECT Any, in a sheltered or exposed position; full sun
to partial shade

SOIL Any fertile, well-drained soil

HARDINESS Fully hardy at temperatures down to
-15°C/5°F; needs no winter protection

DROUGHT TOLERANCE Good, once established

PROBLEMS Vine weevil; powdery mildew

PRUNING Minimal; remove dead or damaged growth in
mid or late spring, and remove any plain green foliage
as it appears, to prevent the plant losing its variegation

PROPAGATION Greenwood cuttings in late spring;
softwood or semi-ripe cuttings in late spring to late
summer; hardwood cuttings from autumn to late winter

Euonymus fortunei 'Silver Queen'

⬆ 2m/6ft ⬌ 90cm/3ft   EASY

A small, bushy shrub easily coaxed into climbing mode, it is grown for its reliable and attractive evergreen foliage. It has dark green leaves with creamy white edging and insignificant pale greenish flowers in summer that are occasionally followed by pale pink berries. If planted against a wall it will naturally begin to incline and climb the wall without the need for garden wires.

> **BEST USES** Ideal for courtyards, entrances, around front doors or growing up low walls; high on focal appeal but low in maintenance

FLOWERS May to June, but grown mainly for foliage
SCENTED No
ASPECT Any, in a sheltered or exposed position; full sun to partial shade
SOIL Any fertile, well-drained soil
HARDINESS Fully hardy at temperatures down to -15°C/5°F; needs no winter protection
DROUGHT TOLERANCE Good, once established
PROBLEMS None
PRUNING Minimal; trim in early spring before new growth appears, and remove any plain green foliage as it appears, to prevent the plant losing its variegation
PROPAGATION Greenwood cuttings in late spring; softwood or semi-ripe cuttings in late spring to late summer; hardwood cuttings from autumn to late winter

••

GREENFINGER TIP *The leaf variegation is stronger when the plant is positioned in full sun*

x *Fatshedera lizei* 🎖

Tree ivy

⬆ 2m/6ft ⬌ 90cm/3ft   EASY

This evergreen shrub is a cross between *Fatsia japonica* and *Hedera helix*. It can be grown as a small climber but, because the growth habit is lax, it will need to be tied into a framework of garden wires from the outset. It has panicles of small, white-greenish flowers in autumn, but it is the large, lustrous, glossy leaves that make this such an appealing climber.

> **BEST USES** Ideal for coastal areas and sheltered gardens, the lush evergreen foliage is perfect for the exotic garden

FLOWERS October, but grown mainly for foliage
SCENTED No
ASPECT East, south or west facing, in a sheltered position; full sun to partial shade
SOIL Any fertile, well-drained soil
HARDINESS Frost hardy at temperatures down to -5°C/23°F; needs winter protection and may not survive severe winters in the coldest areas
DROUGHT TOLERANCE Good, once established
PROBLEMS Leaves are susceptible to frosts, but will recover quickly if the roots are protected from freezing by mulching the base of the plant in winter
PRUNING Minimal; trim in early spring before new growth appears and pinch out the top new shoots to encourage bushier side growth
PROPAGATION Sow seed in autumn or spring; heeled cuttings at any time of the year

Ficus pumila 🏅
Creeping fig

⬆ 4m/13ft ↔ 2.5m/8ft   **MEDIUM**

Commonly seen as a houseplant or in the office, this tender, evergreen self-clinging climber is grown mainly for its foliage. The young leaves are small and heart-shaped, maturing to larger green leaves that bear the small flowers and, sometimes, hairy, purple, pear-shaped fruits.

> **BEST USES** Perfect as wall cover in a sheltered spot, or delightful grown in a container on a warm, sheltered patio; also suitable as a greenhouse or conservatory climber, and very popular as a houseplant

FLOWERS Insignificant or absent; grown for foliage
SCENTED No
ASPECT South or west facing, in a sheltered position with protection from winds; full sun to partial shade
SOIL Any moist, fertile, humus-rich, well-drained soil
HARDINESS Frost hardy at temperatures down to -5°C/23°F; best grown in a conservatory or frost-free greenhouse in colder areas
DROUGHT TOLERANCE Poor
PROBLEMS Mealy bug, red spider mite, scale insect and thrip
PRUNING Minimal; in late winter or early spring, cut out dead, diseased or wayward growth
PROPAGATION Semi-ripe cuttings with bottom heat in summer

Garrya elliptica 'James Roof' 🏅
Silk tassel bush

⬆ 4m/13ft ↔ 4m/13ft   **EASY**

This elegant evergreen shrub is easy to grow and adapts well as a wall climber. It has leathery, dark green leaves and the male plant produces incredibly long, decorative, pendulous tiers of silver-grey catkin-like flowers that hang like silk tassels in late winter and early spring – hence the common name. Tie stems into a framework of wires or trellis to train it as a wall climber.

> **BEST USES** Offers great architectural interest for the back of the border where its long flower tassels look elegant, especially when covered in frost

FLOWERS December to February
SCENTED No
ASPECT Any, in a sheltered position; full sun to partial shade
SOIL Any fertile, well-drained soil
HARDINESS Fully hardy at temperatures down to -15°C/5°F; needs no winter protection
DROUGHT TOLERANCE Excellent, once established
PROBLEMS None
PRUNING Minimal; in spring, remove damaged, crossed or straggling growth and cut out unwanted stems to maintain size and shape
PROPAGATION Semi-ripe cuttings from summer to late autumn

GREENFINGER TIP *Well worth trying in coastal areas as it stands up to salty air remarkably well*

Hardenbergia violacea 🏅
False sarsparilla

⬆ 2.5m/8ft ⬌ 2m/6ft   MEDIUM

Hardenbergia violacea is an evergreen from Australia that is normally used as a ground cover plant but, with its twining woody stems, it works very well as a small climber. It has long, grey-green leathery leaves and pendulous, pea-like violet flowers in winter to spring. It is an almost hardy plant, suitable for growing outdoors in mild areas, but is best grown as a greenhouse or conservatory plant in colder regions. It is a pretty climber at a time of year when there is little else in flower.

BEST USES Needs sheltered, mild, frost-free conditions to see it at its best, and should do well against a low sheltered wall

FLOWERS January to March
SCENTED No
ASPECT South or west facing, in a sheltered position; full sun, though tolerates partial shade
SOIL Any fertile, well-drained soil
HARDINESS Frost hardy at temperatures down to -5°C/23°F; needs winter protection
DROUGHT TOLERANCE Poor
PROBLEMS Aphids and red spider mite when grown in a greenhouse or conservatory
PRUNING Prune lightly after flowering to maintain shape and size
PROPAGATION Sow pre-soaked seed in spring at 20°C/68°F; softwood cuttings in spring and summer

Hedera algeriensis 'Gloire de Marengo' 🏅
(formerly *H. canariensis*)

⬆ 4m/13ft ⬌ 4m/13ft   EASY

This small but vigorous evergreen climbing shrub clings by aerial roots to its supports. It has silver-green leaves with creamy white edgings. Black berries succeed clusters of small yellow-green flowers in autumn, making it an excellent plant for attracting birds into the garden.

BEST USES Excellent for growing over trellis or against a sheltered wall to bring winter interest to the garden; also makes great ground cover in dappled shade

FLOWERS October, but grown mainly for foliage
SCENTED No
ASPECT Any, in a sheltered position with protection from cold winds; full sun to partial shade
SOIL Any fertile, well-drained soil, with a good mulch to help retain moisture in the summer
HARDINESS Young plants are frost hardy at temperatures down to -5°C/23°F, and may need winter protection with fleece; mature plants are fully hardy at temperatures down to -20°C/-4°F
DROUGHT TOLERANCE Good, once established
PROBLEMS Some leaves may be damaged by frost in a severe winter, but it usually recovers well in spring
PRUNING Minimal; cut back in late winter or early spring to help maintain its size and shape
PROPAGATION Softwood cuttings at any time; semi-ripe cuttings of young growth in summer; hardwood cuttings from late summer to late winter; layering at any time

Hedera helix 'Buttercup'

⬆ 2m/6ft ⬌ Unlimited   **EASY**

A lovely self-clinging evergreen ivy that is versatile and needs very little care. It has small, rounded, pale limey-green leaves when grown in full shade, but these are bright golden yellow if planted in full sun. As ivies flower late in the year, they are an ideal pollen source for bees.

> **BEST USES** Great for difficult shaded areas where few other plants will flourish and to cover unsightly low walls; will also do an admirable job in a container in a small, shady courtyard or city garden

FLOWERS October, but grown mainly for foliage

SCENTED No

ASPECT Any, in a sheltered position; full sun to partial shade

SOIL Any fertile, well-drained soil, with a good mulch to help retain moisture in the summer

HARDINESS Frost hardy at temperatures down to -5°C/23°F; may need winter protection

DROUGHT TOLERANCE Good, once established

PROBLEMS None

PRUNING Trim in early spring, before new growth appears; when growing it against a wall, remove straggling, wayward shoots to help retain shape

PROPAGATION Softwood cuttings or layering at any time; semi-ripe cuttings of young growth in summer; hardwood cuttings from late summer to late winter

GREENFINGER TIP *This is undoubtedly one of the easiest true golden ivies around, but it achieves its best colour when planted in a sunny position*

Hedera helix 'Parsley Crested' ⚇

(formerly 'Cristata') Parsley-crested ivy

⬆ 3.5m/12ft ⬌ 2m/6ft   **EASY**

A mid-green, glossy-leaved, evergreen self-clinging ivy with appealing crinkled leaf edges that age to purple in winter. This is a restrained, discreet ivy, modestly performing 365 days of the year and rarely calling for your attention.

> **BEST USES** Ideal for sheltered positions such as at the foot of walls, and the perfect subject for containers, small woodland arbours and shady courtyards; also useful for inaccessible slopes and banks as an evergreen ground cover

FLOWERS Insignificant or absent; grown for evergreen foliage

SCENTED No

ASPECT Any, in a sheltered position with protection from cold winds; full sun to partial shade

SOIL Any moist, humus-rich, well-drained soil; particularly suited to alkaline soils

HARDINESS Frost hardy at temperatures down to -5°C/23°F; may need winter protection

DROUGHT TOLERANCE Good, once established

PROBLEMS None

PRUNING Trim lightly, removing dead or damaged plant material

PROPAGATION Softwood cuttings at any time; semi-ripe cuttings of young growth in summer; hardwood cuttings from late summer to late winter; layering at any time

Hedera helix 'Pedata'
Bird's foot ivy

⬆ 4m/13ft ⬌ 90cm/3ft   EASY

A slow-growing, elegant, self-clinging evergreen ivy whose neat, three-lobed leaves resemble a bird's foot (hence the common name) and are a pretty, metallic dark green with grey and white veining. The flowers are insignificant or absent altogether. The unusual, attractive leaf shape makes this an interesting year-round climber.

BEST USES Excellent for growing against a sheltered wall or in a container for seasonal interest where space is at a premium; also ideal as a ground cover plant, making an evergreen carpet on awkward slopes or banks

FLOWERS Insignificant or absent; grown for evergreen foliage

SCENTED No

ASPECT Any, in a sheltered position with protection from cold winds; full sun to full shade

SOIL Any moist, well-drained soil, with a good mulch to help retain moisture in the summer

HARDINESS Frost hardy at temperatures down to -5°C/23°F; may need shelter from wind and frosts in colder areas

DROUGHT TOLERANCE Good, once established

PROBLEMS None

PRUNING Minimal; trim lightly in spring to retain shape

PROPAGATION Softwood cuttings or layering at any time; semi-ripe cuttings of young growth in summer; hardwood cuttings from late summer to late winter

Jasminum nudiflorum 🎖
Winter jasmine

⬆ 3m/10ft ⬌ 3m/10ft   EASY

This is a lovely, arching, deciduous shrub that can also be trained as a wall climber by tying the stems into a framework of garden wires. The cheerful, fragrant, lemon-yellow flowers brave the winter cold and burst forth on the bare green stems in winter and early spring, before the appearance of the dark green leaves.

BEST USES Can be grown as a shrub, its stems hanging over walls, or trained as a wall climber; the deep green stems look particularly handsome against an old red brick wall

FLOWERS January to March

SCENTED Scented flowers

ASPECT East, south or west facing, in a sheltered position; full sun to partial shade

SOIL Any moist, fertile, well-drained soil; add organic matter before planting

HARDINESS Fully hardy at temperatures down to -15°C/5°F; needs no winter protection

DROUGHT TOLERANCE Good, once established

PROBLEMS Aphids

PRUNING After flowering, cut back to strong buds and train horizontally on wires

PROPAGATION Semi-ripe cuttings in summer; hardwood cuttings in winter

GREENFINGER TIP *This is a great climber for those with wasp allergies as it flowers when there are no bees or wasps about*

Lonicera x *purpusii* 'Winter Beauty' ♉

⬆ 2m/6ft ⬌ 2.5m/8ft   EASY

One of the loveliest but most underrated honeysuckles, ideal for bringing fragrance and flower into the garden in mid-winter. It is deciduous or semi-evergreen, depending on its situation, with a lovely arching habit and dark green oval leaves. From winter to early spring it has profuse clusters of white, lemony-perfumed flowers that have distinctive yellow anthers, borne on bare stems. Berries are rarely produced.

> **BEST USES** Grow against a sheltered, sunny wall, near an entrance or doorway to enjoy the unexpected pleasure of winter perfume

FLOWERS December to March
SCENTED Scented flowers
ASPECT Any, in a sheltered or exposed position; full sun to partial shade
SOIL Any fertile, well-drained soil
HARDINESS Fully hardy at temperatures down to -15°C/5°F; needs no winter protection
DROUGHT TOLERANCE Good, once established
PROBLEMS None
PRUNING In late spring, cut back straggling stems and cut out dead or diseased wood at the base of the plant to encourage new bottom growth
PROPAGATION Semi-ripe cuttings in summer

....

GREENFINGER TIP *This honeysuckle flowers more profusely when sited in full sun*

Clematis napaulensis

⬆ 6m/20ft ⬌ 3m/10ft   EASY

This vigorous tendrilled clematis is not widely grown and I bet I know why: for most of the year it looks pretty much dead. Come October, however, attractive light green foliage suddenly appears, followed by lovely pale, creamy-white pendent flowers with striking purple stamens in winter. A slow starter, but you will wonder how you ever managed the winter garden without it.

> **BEST USES** A splendid and unusual clematis for courtyards and city gardens or warm sunny borders at the foot of a south-facing sheltered wall; grow in a greenhouse or conservatory in very cold regions

FLOWERS December to January
SCENTED No
ASPECT South or west facing, in a sheltered position; full sun
SOIL Any fertile, well-drained soil
HARDINESS Frost hardy at temperatures down to -5°C/23°F; protect with a mulch or fleece in winter
DROUGHT TOLERANCE Poor
PROBLEMS Clematis wilt
PRUNING None
PROPAGATION Internodal semi-ripe cuttings in mid to late summer; layering late summer to early autumn

Hedera colchica 'Dentata Variegata' ♀

↑ 8m/26ft ↔ 4m/13ft   **EASY**

A fast-growing self-clinging evergreen ivy with large leathery leaves, some 15cm/6in across, with green-grey marbling, handsomely edged with creamy margins. It has limey umbels of flowers in autumn, though these can be sparse or absent. Black berries follow the flowers.

> **BEST USES** Brilliant as a ground cover plant, as well as being a very useful climber for adding colour to dull, difficult, shaded areas; a great climber for a north-facing wall or to liven up a shady courtyard

FLOWERS Insignificant or absent; grown for foliage
SCENTED No
ASPECT Any, in a sheltered or exposed position; full sun to partial shade
SOIL Any fertile, well-drained soil, with a good mulch to help retain moisture in the drier summer months
HARDINESS Fully hardy at temperatures down to -10°C/14°F; needs no winter protection
DROUGHT TOLERANCE Excellent, once established
PROBLEMS None
PRUNING Cut back at any time of year, to maintain size and shape
PROPAGATION Softwood cuttings and layering at any time; semi-ripe cuttings of young growth in summer or hardwood cuttings from late summer to late winter

....

GREENFINGER TIP *Insects love this plant, so it is great for wildlife gardens*

Hedera helix 'Oro di Bogliasco'
(formerly 'Goldheart')

↑ 8m/26ft ↔ 3m/10ft   **EASY**

This evergreen climber has small, dark green, heart-shaped leaves which are splashed prettily with creamy gold variegation in the centre and held on pink stems. The plain, greenish flowers are followed by small black berries.

> **BEST USES** Excellent for pergolas, fences and against sound brickwork; like all ivies it is an autumn flowerer, so is very attractive to insects and an ideal choice for a wildlife garden

FLOWERS October to November, but grown mainly for foliage
SCENTED No
ASPECT Any, in a sheltered position protected from cold winds; full sun to partial shade
SOIL Any fertile, well-drained soil, with a good mulch to help retain moisture in the summer
HARDINESS Fully hardy at temperatures down to -10°C/14°F; needs no winter protection
DROUGHT TOLERANCE Excellent, once established
PROBLEMS None
PRUNING Cut back at any time of year, to maintain shape and size
PROPAGATION Softwood cuttings and layering at any time; semi-ripe cuttings of young growth in summer or hardwood cuttings from late summer to late winter

....

GREENFINGER TIP *Although it is fully hardy, juvenile foliage can be caught by frosts, so choose a sheltered site to see it at its best – it will recover*

Hedera colchica 'Dentata' ♀
Bullock's heart ivy

⬆ 10m/32ft ⬌ 3m/10ft   **EASY**

A very appealing, fast-growing evergreen ivy that has long, thin, arching, bright green leaves with attractive purple leaf tips and stems. The greeny umbelled flowers are only produced on mature plants.

BEST USES Great for shaded areas where few other plants will succeed, to cover unsightly structures and as very effective ground cover; don't be afraid to cut back as required

FLOWERS Insignificant or absent; grown for foliage
SCENTED No
ASPECT Any, in a sheltered position; full sun to partial shade
SOIL Any fertile, well-drained soil, with a good mulch to help retain moisture in the drier summer months
HARDINESS Fully hardy at temperatures down to -15°C/5°F; needs no winter protection
DROUGHT TOLERANCE Excellent, once established
PROBLEMS None
PRUNING Cut back in spring to restrict shape and size
PROPAGATION Softwood cuttings and layering at any time; semi-ripe cuttings of young growth in summer or hardwood cuttings from late summer to late winter

....

GREENFINGER TIP *Keep moist in hot weather, and prune to prevent its weight getting so heavy that it destabilises walls and fences*

Hedera colchica 'Sulphur Heart' ♀
(formerly 'Paddy's Pride') Persian ivy

⬆ 10m/32ft ⬌ 3m/10ft   **EASY**

This striking, self-clinging evergreen ivy has a rapid growth rate with attractive, large, dark green glossy leaves, splotched with creamy yellow splashes in the centre and appealing lime-green edging. It has plain green spherical flowers. It needs sturdy supports as the leaf mass can get quite heavy (and make sure your wall has sound mortar joints).

BEST USES Grows well in difficult areas, making good ground cover; like all ivies, it attracts pollinating insects, so is a valuable addition to the wildlife garden

FLOWERS October to November, but grown mainly for foliage
SCENTED No
ASPECT Any, in a sheltered position; full sun to partial shade
SOIL Any fertile, well-drained soil, with a good mulch to help retain moisture in the summer
HARDINESS Fully hardy at temperatures down to -15°C/5°F; needs no winter protection
DROUGHT TOLERANCE Excellent, once established
PROBLEMS None
PRUNING Cut back to maintain size and shape in spring, or as needed
PROPAGATION Softwood cuttings and layering at any time; semi-ripe cuttings of young growth in summer or hardwood cuttings from late summer to late winter

....

GREENFINGER TIP *Too much shade will reduce the variegation in the leaves*

Hedera helix
Common ivy, English ivy

⬆ 12m/40ft ⬌ 8m/26ft   **EASY**

This rampant, self-clinging evergreen climber has a colossal growth habit and should be sold with a large red danger sign attached! Admittedly it has handsome, glossy leathery leaves that are a uniform dark green and small green flower umbels in autumn, which are followed by black berries. However, it respects no man-made boundaries and will annex everything in your garden should you be foolish enough to plant it.

BEST USES Marvellous for covering long stretches of concrete fencing, where nothing else will grow, or as evergreen ground cover in woodland

FLOWERS September to October, but grown mainly for foliage

SCENTED No

ASPECT Any, in a sheltered or exposed position; full sun to full shade

SOIL Any fertile, well-drained soil

HARDINESS Fully hardy at temperatures down to -15°C/5°F; needs no winter protection

DROUGHT TOLERANCE Excellent, once established

PROBLEMS Extremely, extremely invasive

PRUNING Cut back at any time of year, to restrict size

PROPAGATION Softwood cuttings and layering at any time; semi-ripe cuttings of young growth in summer or hardwood cuttings from late summer to late winter

Hedera hibernica ♛
Irish ivy

⬆ 10–12m/32–38ft ⬌ 8m/26ft   **EASY**

An elegant evergreen ivy with dense, plain green leaves that are often flushed an attractive bronze in winter and have distinctive lobing at the edges. The umbels of green flowers attract pollinating insects in autumn and are followed by trusses of black berries in winter. It will need sturdy support and regular cutting back to prevent its weight pulling against walls and fences.

BEST USES Ideal for difficult shady areas and to cover unsightly structures, where few other plants will flourish, and a reliable ground cover plant

FLOWERS October to November, but grown mainly for foliage

SCENTED No

ASPECT Any, in a sheltered or exposed position; full sun to light shade

SOIL Any fertile, well-drained soil, with a good mulch to help retain moisture in the summer

HARDINESS Fully hardy at temperatures down to -15°C/5°F; needs no winter protection

DROUGHT TOLERANCE Excellent, once established

PROBLEMS None

PRUNING Cut back to maintain size and shape in spring, or as needed

PROPAGATION Softwood cuttings and layering at any time; semi-ripe cuttings of young growth in summer or hardwood cuttings from late summer to late winter

Supports

All climbing plants can support themselves to a greater or lesser degree, and some, such as ivy, can make their way upwards with no help at all. Others are going to require assistance from man-made supports.

Climbers may require support because they need something to cling to or twine round, or because they cannot support their own weight when mature. The method by which a plant climbs, and its ultimate size, will together give a good indication of what growing supports are suitable.

How plants climb

Self-clinging stem roots

Self-clinging climbers need no help at all. Ivy is the most common climber that uses self-clinging roots to aid its climbing ambitions. As well as travelling vertically, it will also creep horizontally across the ground, making excellent ground cover. It doesn't mind that there are no garden wires, pergolas or other typical structures for it to climb because it has developed small, but incredibly effective, aerial roots which allow it to cling to almost any rough surface.

Ivy is legendary for the destruction it can cause by attaching itself to damaged masonry and crumbling brick mortar joints; this has given it a rather bad reputation. However, there are some places in the garden where almost nothing will grow, and it is here that ivy becomes indispensable. There are many varieties more considerate in their growing temperament than the ruthless common ivy (*Hedera helix*) and these are really worth your consideration; examples include *H.h.* 'Oro di Bogliasco' (formerly 'Goldheart') with heart-shaped leaves splashed gold in the centre or the more diminutive, but no less charming, bird's-foot ivy (*H.h.* 'Pedata').

Adhesive pads

Virginia creeper (*Parthenocissus quinquefolia*) and Boston ivy (*P. tricuspidata*) have stem tendrils with the added benefit of adhesive pads at the tips, so they can effectively clasp any vertical or horizontal elevation: they can be seen suckering their way across the ground as commonly as climbing skyward. Plants that climb in this fashion often only need a small bamboo support to get them started and are pretty much self-clinging as they grow.

Leaf tendrils

Some plants climb by clinging to other stems of the same plant or grasping the stems of surrounding plants, including the branches of neighbouring trees or shrubs, using modified leaves called leaf tendrils. They will naturally grow towards any available support, wires or trellis.

Clematis, Chilean glory vine (*Eccremocarpus scaber*), nasturtiums (*Tropaeolum*), sweet peas (*Lathyrus*) and the cup and saucer vine (*Cobaea scandens*) all use tendrils to attach themselves to whatever is nearby. Although these tendrils look quite fragile, don't be fooled: they are incredibly strong, wiry apparatus and effective in assisting the plant to elevate and insinuate itself above the opposition.

With the exception of some of the clematis, none of these climbers reach any great height or weight, so they only need modest support, such as bamboo canes lashed together to form a framework or tying in to garden wires or trellis. (The more rampant clematis may need more support.)

Stem tendrils

Stem tendrils are shoots that grow out from the stem, reaching out into the air until they find something they can grasp. Passionflower (*Passiflora*) and grape vine (*Vitis*) climb in this way. These climbers need strong, sturdy

A variety of climbing techniques: (*left*) clematis tendrils twining upwards on trellis; (*centre*) the adhesive pads of ivy stick firmly to a fence panel; (*right*) slender clematis leaf tendrils use bamboo supports to aid their upward climb

structures, such as a timber pergola or a large grid of heavy-duty galvanised wires, fixed by vine eyes into a sound wall, to fully support the climber as it matures and develops the greater weight of full leaf (which can act much like a sail in high winds), fruits or flowers.

Twining stems

Some plants climb by twining their stems: they will wind them tightly around a climbing apparatus or the natural support provided by trees and shrubs. Plants that use this method include wisteria, morning glory (*Ipomoea*), jasmine, honeysuckle (*Lonicera*) and Dutchman's pipe (*Aristolochia macrophylla*).

A newly planted climber will have juvenile stems and foliage, but the stems of many of these climbers thicken and become woody as they mature. This helps the plant support the weight of new growth, flowers and fruits, which can be considerable, but also indicates the need for a strong support structure. However, annual climbers and those that never attain a great height will not need the hefty supports required by larger climbers.

Scramblers and ramblers

The tendril climbers and twiners will happily climb upwards, needing only a little assistance at the outset to get them heading in a vertical direction, while other climbers need rather more help to stay upright. Climbing roses employ a plethora of grasping hooks – thorns to you and me – so they can ramble and heave themselves upwards. (Unlikely though it may seem, the thorns or prickles on a rose stem are actually modified leaves, thought to have evolved to protect the plant from the unwelcome interest of scavenging animals.)

Cape leadwort (*Plumbago*) and bougainvillea are scramblers. They use neighbouring plants in a sort of piggyback mode to assist them in their upwardly mobile activities. Like the ramblers, they will need to be tied on to a strong support at regular intervals or they risk becoming an impenetrable snarled heap on the ground.

Wall shrubs as climbers

Many of the plants that we usually grow as stand-alone ornamental shrubs can also be grown as climbers. As ornamentals they add a focal point to a mixed border and, left to their own devices, will form spreading, arching or weeping shrubs, needing only occasional pruning to keep them looking neat and tidy. The beauty of some of these shrubs is that, because they are fairly pliable in their growth pattern, they can be trained to clothe a small wall or form a small hedge. This is particularly useful when they have special features such as attractive evergreen or variegated foliage, or interesting berries.

In its natural state, euonymus forms a neat, small, mounded shrub. But if you take a young euonymus such as *E. fortunei* 'Silver Queen' and position it against a wall, it will naturally grow upwards, with only light pruning here and there needed to keep it on a vertical track. *Cotoneaster horizontalis* behaves in a similar way. By encouraging the plant to grow up the wall, rather than leaving it to go its own way, an ornamental shrub is transformed into a wall-clothing climber.

Some shrubs readily lend themselves to wall-climbing, as their juvenile stems are pliable and are easily tied horizontally. These include quince (*Chaenomeles*), spindle bush (*Euonymus*) and California lilacs (*Ceanothus*). Other shrubs will not adapt to this method at all: their stems are stiff and unbending and would certainly split or break if you attempted to train them. Trellis or vine eyes and garden wires fixed firmly to a garden wall are sufficient support, and using soft garden twine to tie the stems to the wires will avoid damage to the growing shoots or stems. The trick is to cut away any stem that is not growing in formation or is straggling sideways.

Solanum crispum on a wooden trellis covering a bare wall

Growing climbers on man-made supports

Bare walls and fences

Walls and fences are obvious supports for climbing plants, yet they are surprisingly often overlooked: they are already in existence, sturdy and cheap! If you have bare walls and fences in your garden, you have the luxury of a lot of growing space to fill and they are the ideal places to grow dramatic, colourful climbers.

Walls and fences absorb heat and will increase the temperature in that specific area of the garden slightly, providing a sheltered habitat or microclimate. If they are fairly sheltered and facing south or west, you could consider growing some of the less

Formal garden with obelisks as focal points

hardy plants and annual climbers, such as Chilean glory flower (*Eccremocarpus scaber*), Cape leadwort (*Plumbago auriculata*) or creeping fig (*Ficus pumila*).

Attaching trellis to a wall is a popular way of providing support for climbing plants, and there is a huge choice of finishes and sizes available. Trellis has the added advantage of looking smart even in winter, when your climbers are reduced to nothing more than bare stems. When fixing trellis to the wall, it is sensible to mount it on wooden battens to create a gap between the trellis and the wall: this ensures good air circulation around the plant, which will help to reduce diseases.

A second option is to fix galvanised or plastic-coated wires to fencing or walls. These can be attached using screw and drive vine eyes or tension bolts. When fixing vine eyes into the wall or fence, place them no more than 2m/6ft apart, with the first line 45cm/18in above ground level, as this is low enough to allow the climber to first attach itself to its climbing support. Position the others at 30–45cm/12–18in apart, and

stretch the support wires horizontally, ensuring they are tightly tensioned and secured. When securing wires along panelled fencing it is very easy to fix the wires to the fence posts using galvanised staples.

Always use soft string or garden twine when tying climbing plants to supports, whether trellis or wire, to prevent damage to the plant itself.

Free-standing climbing structures

When choosing a frame to support climbing plants, one of your first considerations should be the shape, size and strength of the frame, depending on what you are thinking of growing on it. Gardeners often overlook the weight of mature plants: the spindly structures that were more than adequate when the climber was newly planted may not be strong enough as it becomes taller, heavier and wider. So always make provision for the plant's ultimate size and weight. This is

Sweet peas tangle round their wigwam support

beautifully crafted that they stand up as focal points in their own right, and you might even decide against growing any sort of climber up them at all.

The style of your garden will also play a part. Do you favour traditional willow or natural wood structures, or is your garden more contemporary, requiring a shiny stainless steel or tubular architectural composition?

Arches and pergolas

Pergolas and garden arches give sturdy support to climbing plants; they also offer a focal point in any garden. They are something interesting to look at in mid-winter, even when only covered with bare winter stems touched by a magical, sparkling hard frost (who can deny that a snow-covered archway in the depths of winter has a unique, still beauty all its own?) and can make a dramatic statement in any space.

They can also be useful. A timber pergola used as a walkway from one part of the garden to another is a wonderful means of linking areas, even when your climbers aren't in bloom, and arches can frame the entrance to even the tiniest garden. Don't just consider the obvious solutions. A very attractive and effective way of displaying climbing roses informally might be through a series of scalloped rope swags, encircling a sitting area or acting as a floral division between one part of the garden and another. I've done this myself and added a golden hop (*Humulus lupulus* 'Aureus') to the mix: after the gorgeous extravagance of perfumed roses, I still had the ornamental hops to enjoy, hanging languorously in the early autumn sunlight.

When planning an overhead structure of any kind, it is a common mistake to allow insufficient height once it is fully clothed with plants. It must be tall enough so that you can walk comfortably through it without dodging

particularly true of climbers whose stems become woody with age, such as wisteria.

A second consideration is the purpose the structure will serve. An arbour can provide dappled shade in which to relax and read a book; a pergola draped with a large romantic vine will create an outside dining area with a Mediterranean atmosphere. Trellis is an effective screen for the unsightly area where the rubbish bins are stored; a well-placed obelisk can add vertical interest in the flower beds. There are a great many very attractive garden supports, so

Good companions

• Honeysuckles and roses are a classic cottage garden combination and rarely fail to please. *Rosa* 'New Dawn' pairs very prettily with many of the white, mid-pink or dark purple clematis. Try to choose a clematis that flowers at much the same time as your chosen rose. If you are really clever, plant one of the later-flowering clematis, such as the rich purple *C.* 'Venosa Violacea', which will flower from July to September, and with any luck you'll have an almost non-stop flowering display all year.

• If you are a keen veggie grower, any of the dark purple-flowering summer clematis, such as *C.* 'Gipsy', make a refreshing union, glancing alluringly through the fresh green foliage of climbing beans. The autumnal tints and dozing bells of any autumn-flowering clematis such as *C. texensis* or *C. tangutica* prove a charming addition, threading through the late-flowering pale buff hops of the glorious golden ornamental hop (*Humulus lupulus* 'Aureus').

• *Ipomoea tricolor* 'Heavenly Blue' is an attractive annual climber which proves unerringly handy for clothing the bare lower limbs of yellow shrub roses, such as climbing *Rosa* 'Golden Showers'. Any of the sweet peas can be planted with small climbing roses or shrub roses: *Lathyrus latifolius* tangled in amongst the shrub rose 'Iceberg' makes a charming combination. This happy pairing has the added benefit of providing delightful cut flowers for the house.

• Herbaceous clematis create an appealing floral tapestry when allowed to scramble through surrounding perennial plants or grasses. (You should treat herbaceous clematis as you would other herbaceous plants, cutting them back to 15cm/6in above ground level in late autumn or early spring.) These gorgeous clematis don't achieve any great height, but they do look exceptionally charming lacing their way through low-growing plants. Despite being less familiar to gardeners than climbing clematis, they are definitely well worth consideration. The deep velvety indigo *C.* x *durandii* always makes an impression weaving through a swathe of *Stipa arundinacea* (now known as *Anemanthele lessioniana*) or tactile cotton lavender (*Santolina pinnata* subsp. *neapolitana*). You might also consider a tumbling partnership of the pale pinky purple nodding flowers of *Clematis* 'Rosea' with any miniature patio or shrub roses or the hardy blue, purple or white geraniums.

• *Rosa banksiae* is one of the best companions to grow through any of the wisterias, being mighty enough to compete with their vigorous growth rate. Yellow always complements the mauve, blue and white species especially well.

a large tangle of hostile, thorny rose stems! Even if you are short, you will surely have taller garden visitors. The upright posts need to be a minimum of 2.5m/8ft above the ground to accommodate the burgeoning plants as they grow, and any structure of this kind must be sturdy, to withstand the weight of the plants in maturity and to stand firmly against any strong, prevailing winds. Always make sure that you site any arch or pergola so that generous planting holes can be dug at the footings.

Obelisks, wigwams and bamboo frames
Obelisks are a great way of bringing height into a flower border and an ideal way to display some of the smaller climbers. These come in a variety of finishes, from verdigris metal to powder-coated tubular steel, galvanised or wrought iron and contemporary stainless steel. Less expensive alternatives include natural hazel or willow wigwams that concertina apart, providing a more traditional style of garden structure. Bamboo is cheap and versatile and looks quite at home in the informal cottage garden. A tepee of canes tied together can be placed over a large container to show off your summer sweet peas. Add one of the dwarf climbing clematis to these and you have a pretty floral focal point at very little cost.

Growing climbers through trees and shrubs

Trees and shrubs provide a natural, no-cost framework for climbing plants. However, it can be difficult to get a timid climber to scramble up a vigorous, fast-growing tree or shrub, as one will probably out-do the other. The key to success is to be realistic about what you plant: although it is well nigh impossible to train a climber up a large oak tree, for example, some of the smaller conifers and evergreen hedges take to companion climbers incredibly well.

Ivy is a tough competitor to team with other climbers because of its vigorous nature: common ivy will pitilessly swamp any competition. Climbing hydrangea (*Hydrangea anomala* subsp. *petiolaris*) copes very well with some of the less rampant ivy varieties, displaying its panicles of creamy flowers before the ivy takes over with their attractive limey flower heads. Recommended ivy varieties that are not too vigorous include *Hedera colchica* 'Dentata Variegata', with attractive cream-edged leaves, or try the lovely golden-leaved *H. helix* 'Buttercup', which reaches no more than 2m/6ft in height.

Rosa filipes 'Kiftsgate' is a beautiful white rose that gets up to 10m/32ft or more. It's a bit of a giant, but if allowed the freedom to climb through, say, a big old apple tree, you will get the benefit of the apple blossom in spring, with the added spectacle of a tumble of white roses later in the summer. It's not much good if you decide to plant the same rose in a small flower bed, up a tiny pergola or over a small low fence, because 'Kiftsgate' will simply grow like the clappers and quickly smother its neighbours.

Trees and shrubs invariably have a period after flowering when they become a sombre, brooding mass of monotonous green, and climbers are a perfect booster for jazzing them up a bit. By combining them with other plants, trees or shrubs, climbers will effectively extend the season of garden interest. A dull laurel hedge or scrappy privet can be clothed in a mass of flowers by adding a colourful climber such as honeysuckle. Try *Lonicera periclymenum* 'Belgica' or *L.p.* 'Serotina', which unfailingly work their fragrant flowering magic in transforming a boring old hedge. Other honeysuckles, such as *Lonicera x italica*, are more moderate in growth, but still do a marvellous job of breathing new life into dull hedging with prolific scented summer flowers and berries in autumn.

The fiery flame red of *Tropaeolum speciosum* looks incredibly striking when grown through dark green shrubs and hedges, such as azalea, camellia or yew. Deep greens and reds are always a winning colour combination in a yuletidey festive sort of way. If you can persuade the Scots flame flower (as *T. speciosum* is sometimes known) to grow up the impossible *leylandii* (and believe me with a little coaxing it can be done), you can almost feel something approaching fondness for this ghastly conifer.

Clematis flammula, with fragrant, starry white flowers, or the equally perfumed, white-flowered *C. vitalba* are both charming when allowed to grow over any small to medium-sized evergreen or deciduous shrub or hedge. With flowers followed by attractive seed heads, they really prolong the visual impact of a shrub that has long passed its best. Many of the deep-coloured clematis look superb tangled with the sultry smoke bush, *Cotinus coggyria* 'Royal Purple', or indeed any purple, bronzed or golden-leaved shrubs. Spring-flowering shrubs such as *Exochorda* x *macrantha* 'The Bride' look fresh and eye-catching when planted with any of the early-flowering clematis, such as pale blue *C.* 'Frances Rivis'.

Aspect

Sun and shade

When standing with your back to the wall of your house, which way do you (and your garden) face? The direction is referred to as the garden's aspect. Gardens with a south-facing aspect will be in full sun all day (provided, of course, that the sun is out), while gardens that face north will receive only indirect sunlight or be in shade for much of the day, and are often damp spaces. Gardens that face east get light in the mornings, and west-facing gardens get all the afternoon and evening sun.

Some plants need full sun to grow at their best, whilst others may be happier in light shade, but all, without exception, need a certain amount of indirect or direct sunlight to survive. Therefore it's important to be aware of your garden's aspect when choosing plants so you can match them to a suitable planting spot.

City gardens, even if they are west or south facing, can still have sunlight blocked by neighbouring buildings or tall trees casting shade, so may not receive as many hours of sunlight as a rural garden in an open position with no obstacles impeding sunlight. North-facing spaces receive so little sunlight that they are notorious trouble spots. The number of plants that can thrive in full shade is limited, but many can cope

Hydrangea anomala subsp. *petiolaris* covering a shady brick wall and framing the entrance to a garden walkway

Sun-loving *Clematis* 'Princess Diana'

take the full force of extreme weather, both cold and hot.

An area that is blasted by chilly north winds is no place for a sun-loving clematis or exotic climber. Some plants resent winds of any kind and like to be in a toasty hot spot, protected from the more inclement effects of the weather. The base of a sunny wall will invariably have warmer soil at its footings, and rarely be exposed to any winds at all, providing a suitable environment for a less hardy plant that would not survive elsewhere in the garden. In any garden, there are usually areas that have their own microclimates of this kind so make good use of them.

You may be lucky enough to have a brick-walled garden, or a garden space enclosed by fencing, hedges or mature trees and shrubs. These boundaries will give shelter from strong, cold or drying winds or gales. Seaside gardeners can struggle to grow many common garden plants because of adverse coastal conditions, including salt-laden winds (see page 105). One way to increase the range of plants that will grow in this hostile environment is to provide shelter planting: growing hedges or installing man-made screens as a windbreak, specifically sited to filter out the harshest of the wind elements that can be so incredibly destructive to plant establishment. The fence or hedge will divert winds from the lower growing perennials or climbers planted within the shelter of the sanctuary.

In milder regions and city centres, frost is not going to be a major anxiety, but for those who live in colder rural areas, hard frosts can be an almost nightly occurrence in winter. Greenhouses, polytunnels and conservatories all offer a contrived sheltered environment in which to grow plants that cannot withstand the harsher elements of our native climate. Cloches and cold frames will provide more limited protection (see page 107).

with some shade, though their flowering is often very much reduced. These include many of the honeysuckles and specifically *Rosa* 'Zéphirine Drouhin' (see page 125 for further suggestions). Sun-loving climbers include bougainvillea, many clematis, actinidia, sweet peas, cobaea and roses to name but a few. *Clematis* 'Nelly Moser' will fry in full sun; other clematis love their heads in the sun, but need their roots in the shade.

East-facing walls have their own problems. If planted on an east-facing wall, wisterias may have their flower buds frosted overnight, only to be scorched by the rising sun as it thaws them. The result is damaged flower buds that will flower poorly or not at all.

Shelter

Gardens with exposed aspects are wide open to the elements, with little shelter from winds, frost, rain and snow. They are also areas that have little protection from direct overhead sunlight and warm, drying winds in the summer months, so these gardens will

Soil

Plants need soil to grow. It anchors a plant in the ground and provides all the essential nutrients, air and water it needs. These essentials are taken up by the plant's roots and used by the plant to form flowers and leaves. Understanding your soil and knowing how to improve it will make a big difference to the quality of your plants. Soil is the linchpin of any garden: good soil makes good plants. The better your soil, the stronger, healthier and more attractive your plants will be.

Depending on their composition, garden soils can vary greatly in their ability to absorb water and in their fertility, which will have a direct impact on how well or poorly any garden plants grow. A good soil is:

- **moist** – able to retain water, without ever becoming boggy
- **fertile** – rich in nutrients and able to support new plant growth
- **well drained** – allowing excess surface water to drain away
- **crumbly and open in texture** (if it is similar to a good apple crumble mix when you handle it, you've got a pretty good soil!)

Sadly, nature does not endow every garden with the perfect soil, but there are ways of improving its quality. Whilst it may never achieve the crumbly richness of a natural loam, which is the most coveted garden soil of all, you can go a long way to transforming your garden soil into something approaching the ideal.

Feeding the soil

There is a difference between feeding the soil and feeding your plants. Feeding your soil, and thereby improving its structure, will in turn feed and nurture your plants. Feeding your plants with chemical fertilisers will feed the plant directly when applied, but it will not provide any short- or long-term benefit to the composition or texture of your garden soil.

Soil is made up of a mixture of organic matter (or humus) and minerals; the organic matter is the decomposed remains of plants, animals and insects, and the minerals come from the underlying layers of rock in the ground. If you have sandy garden soil that is low in nutrients, or lumpy, sticky clay with poor drainage, your plants will not grow as well as they might.

The texture, drainage and nutrient values of your soil can all be improved by digging in organic matter such as well-rotted farmyard manure or home-made garden compost. Applied annually, over a period of years, this added matter will work wonders. As your soil is enriched with humus, it will slowly become endowed with all the qualities of ideal soil.

On clay and chalk soils, it is easiest to apply this on the surface as a mulch (see page 108) in autumn, allowing winter cold and frost to break it down so it is more workable in the spring, and happily saving you the bother of digging it in. Let the earthworms do their thing – they are wonderful natural composters! On sand or loam soils, dig it in, in late winter or early spring: on a light soil this is hardly the arduous task it becomes on heavier soils and it won't get washed away as it might if left on the surface.

Types of soil

Clay is harder work than most soils, because it is wet and heavy in winter but becomes rock hard during times of drought. A simple test to determine whether your garden soil is clay is to take a small lump and roll it into a ball in the palm of your hands. If it turns into a sticky, damp globe, you have clay soil.

It can be a difficult soil to garden on, becoming either too wet or too dry to dig. It is also known as a 'cold' soil, as it is slow to warm up in spring. And the digging itself is hard going because the soil is quite a weight (Geoff Hamilton used to reckon you could always spot a clay gardener as they were more sturdily built than the wand-like loam or sandy-soiled gardeners!).

The upside is that clay is high in nutrients and, whilst it is slow to warm up in the spring, it retains warmth well throughout the growing season. Roses are particularly happy in clay, as are the majority of the climbers mentioned in this book.

Sandy soil is light and dry (or 'free-draining'), containing less than 10 per cent of clay and mostly made up of very small particles of silica and quartz. It warms up much earlier in the year than other soils, but the nutritional content of sandy soil is usually poor and it needs to be constantly 'beefed up' with organic matter, both to improve available plant food nutrients and to help the soil retain moisture.

You'll know if you have sandy soil because it is very thin and granular and will run through your fingers like, well, sand! Many grasses and silver-leaved plants, and a good range of climbers, are very happy in sandy soil.

Loam is the caviar of soils. It is a rich, dark brown, with a crumbly texture, and has all the good points of clay and sandy soil combined, without any of the disadvantages: it is easily worked, holds moisture well, has high nutrient levels and good drainage. Because of its texture, plant roots become easily established. It is the most coveted of all growing mediums and the type of soil most gardeners strive for, as it makes life so easy!

Chalky or calcareous soils are invariably lacking in fertility and humus and the main task here is to introduce as much organic matter as possible into the soil annually. Underlying these soils are chalk or limestone, which means they are very free-draining and often bone dry in summer. Conversely, they can be sticky and difficult to work on in wet weather. Chalk prevents plant roots absorbing nutrients efficiently, and the number of plants that thrive in this type of soil is limited, though many honeysuckles will do well on chalk.

Peat is not as common as the other soils and is largely found in the east of England, in the fens and low-lying lands that have been reclaimed from marshlands. It is easily recognisable by its almost black colour, and is the result of the decay of plant material over thousands of years.

This type of soil is absolutely lime-free and contains a high percentage of humus. It is an excellent medium for growing acid-loving plants, such as azaleas and rhododendrons, and is an easy soil to manage and dig. It feels almost spongy to the touch, and its disadvantage is that it may be waterlogged in winter but then dries out very quickly in summer.

Many plants can grow happily on a wide variety of soils, but others are much more specific in their soil requirements. Some prefer an acid soil. These plants hate lime (calcium carbonate) in their diet because it prevents them absorbing the full range of nutrients from the soil that they require to grow well. They may not die instantly because of this aversion, but they will have a shorter life expectancy. They often become chlorotic (their leaves yellowing) and will almost certainly never achieve the desired size or enjoy the vigorous new growth they

The pendent flowers of acid-loving *Berberidopsis corallina*

Growing

This is the exciting part. Once your garden structure is in place, you can begin buying your climbers and planting them.

Buying

When purchasing any plant, the main thing to look for is vigorous healthy growth. Plants with leaves that are yellowed or discoloured should be dismissed. Press the top of the soil in the pot to see that it is moist and well watered, but do not buy if it is waterlogged. Similarly, avoid those that are bone dry – a sure sign that the garden centre or nursery has not been looking after their plants as well as they should. If you see roots straddling over the sides of the pots or matting through the drainage holes in the base of the pot, keep looking until you find a better specimen.

Planting

Generally speaking, climbers can be planted at any time of the year provided the soil is not too wet or frozen. Deciduous plants will be bereft of leaves from late autumn to early spring, but they can still be planted out into their final flowering positions.

If you are hoping to train a climber up a wall or to grow it in conjunction with an established tree or shrub, it is wise to plant the climber an absolute minimum of 30cm/12in and up to 3–4ft/1–1.2m from the base of the wall or tree. The soil will be more fertile and you will avoid the tree roots and concrete footings near the surface which make digging a satisfactory hole difficult. Always ensure that there will be plenty of space for them to grow into once planted.

Dig a hole that comfortably accommodates the climber of your choice. The

would in a compatible soil environment. Similarly, plants that are lime-lovers, such as clematis, may suffer growth setbacks in acutely acidic soil. Well-known acid-loving shrubs include azalea, rhododendron and camellia, holly and pieris, and heathers (known as *Erica*, hence the term 'ericaceous' for acid-loving plants). Some climbers will do well in an acid soil. These include the coral plant (*Berberidopsis corallina*), celastrus and campsis.

A simple soil testing kit, available from garden centres, will give a reliable indication of the acidity or alkalinity levels (measured as pH) in your garden soil. Acid soil has a pH below 7, while alkaline soil has a pH above 7. Generally speaking, most plants will grow at their best in a soil with a neutral pH of 7.

Always try to choose a plant that suits all aspects of your soil, including its acidity or alkalinity. You are making an awful lot of work for yourself when you choose to grow plants that prefer an acid soil if your garden is mainly clay. Although it is possible to increase the alkalinity of a soil by adding lime, or to buy ericaceous compost specially formulated for growing acid-loving plants in containers, it is a lot simpler to stick to the plants that will be happy in your existing conditions. Choose the right plant in the first place.

easiest thing to do is to lower the plant whilst still in its container into your planting hole and you will soon appreciate if the hole is the right size. Most climbers are planted so that the soil in the pot is level with that of the garden border, but when planting clematis it is imperative to plant them so that the rootball and the crown of the plant are approximately 10cm/4in below soil level: from experience, most of the common problems that occur with clematis arise because they have not been planted deeply enough in the first place.

At the foot of a wall or fence, or at the base of a tree, the soil is likely to be dry, lacking in nutrients and generally poor, so always water your plant before planting. I like to soak the entire root ball in a bucket of water for about half an hour, but a thorough dunking just before planting will do just as well if time is short. Add a little well-rotted manure or garden compost to the bottom of the planting hole and then tap your plant out of its pot. It helps to gently tease or loosen the roots of most climbers before planting (though it is wiser not to disturb the roots of many of the hybrid clematis). Backfill your hole with soil, adding a handful of peat or bonemeal to improve the nutrient values, then firm the soil around the base of the plant with your hands or heel and water well.

Climbers are usually sold with a support of bamboo already in place, and there is no reason to remove this from the climber when planting. Angle the plant and support cane towards the object you wish it to climb. It should take a month or two for the roots to establish properly. If you have pets, you may want to surround the plant with a protective sleeve of polycarbonate or chicken mesh, to allow it to establish undisturbed.

When growing climbers up large shrubs and trees, ensure that the chosen plant will not overpower the host or that it is so retiring in its growth habit that it cannot compete with its more vigorous planting companions (see page 98). Many clematis and roses are ideal for this purpose and wisteria works incredibly well for growing up larger trees.

A newly planted climber is going to need a little help to establish when planted near a strong, mature tree. The tree will absorb most of the available water and nutrients, so it is vitally important to nurture the climber with regular feed and water to help it get up and away. Don't worry that it doesn't scramble up the tree in the first year. The easiest solution is to drive a stake into the edge of the planting hole, attach garden twine, galvanised wire or a plastic chain to it and secure this to the lower branches of the tree: this is all the encouragement it will need to bridge the gap.

Climbers in pots and containers

Annual climbers are ideal for growing in pots and containers. An annual plant is one that achieves its full life cycle, from seed to plant and flowers, in the space of one season, and they are a breeze for first-time growers (see page 117). Examples include sweet peas (*Lathyrus*), cup and saucer vine (*Cobaea scandens*) and morning glory (*Ipomoea*). Many will self-seed, reappearing the following year without further aid from the gardener. As they are fairly lightweight in their growth habit and die back at the year's end, bamboo tepees, obelisks or willow cones will provide them with all the support they need.

There are also many varieties of perennial climber that have been bred by commercial growers especially for container gardening. New dwarf climbers are showcased at national flower shows every year and there is a huge variety to choose from. Some of these never reach more than 2m/6ft in height, so they are very manageable in a small garden or city patio or balcony. *Clematis* 'Frances Rivis' or the divinely wine-coloured *C.* 'Purple Spider' will thrill many a container gardener. Some of the smaller-leaved, less rampant ivies are also fabulous plants for containers or pots as they provide interest all year round. If you are feeling creative, you can insert a wire structure over a pot and topiarise it, adding extra height and formal elegance in a small or shaded courtyard.

Most climbers, with the exception of the very largest, will survive well in pots or containers as long as they are fed, watered and tended regularly. Choose a suitably sized pot and make sure it has been drilled with drainage holes. Cover these with some crocks (old broken flower pots) and fill with compost, preferably one that is soil-based rather than full of peat, as a peat-based compost will dry out more quickly and is not so rich in nutrients. Plant your chosen climber, firming the soil well with your hands around the base of the plant, so that it makes good contact with the compost, and water it amply.

Clematis are ideal for growing in containers on small patios

The nutrition in the soil will be used up by the plants annually and will need replenishing. This can easily be done by adding a top dressing of used mushroom compost, a dose of liquid fertiliser, or a handful of pelleted chicken manure scattered on the surface, where it will slowly release nutrients into the soil as it breaks down. Check the surface of the pot at least once a week, and water regularly.

Perennial climbers grown in pots will always be restricted in their root growth, and this will limit the size of the ultimate top-growth, so don't expect a climber with a potential height of, say, 8m/26ft to reach that size if it is being grown in a patio container. But that's one of the wonderful things about growing climbers in containers: you can actually tailor them to suit your space.

Coastal gardening

Gardeners who live on the coast or near the sea have to deal with physical challenges such as hostile, salt-laden winds, light, erosive soils and even invasion of their garden spaces by seawater. These conditions are among the most difficult to combat and plants that survive with ease in other areas will struggle or die when faced with such unrelenting weather conditions. Planting a shelter belt will probably be essential (see page 100).

Without underestimating the difficulties of growing in seaside gardens, there are some advantages: the risk of frost is often much lower, so some of the more tender plants can be grown; and there may be less cloud cover than inland, giving more hours of direct light.

There are numerous perennials and shrubs that can cope with these extremes of weather, but few of them are climbers. None the less, there are a few valiant climbing plants which are more than willing to bloom and grow at the seaside (see pages 125–6).

Hardiness

Plant hardiness ratings are judged by different world temperature zones, but in the UK we generally use the RHS hardiness zones, which are explained here. Low temperatures can prevent certain plants from developing well; flower buds may fail to open, and leaves may fall prematurely. If the temperature drops below the plant's level of tolerance for any length of time, it will need some form of protection to prevent lasting damage.

Fully hardy: hardy to -15°C/5°F

This term describes climbers, perennials, shrubs, trees and fruit and vegetables that are naturally tough enough to withstand a lowest winter temperature of -15°C/5°F without suffering lasting harm. No extra mollycoddling from your good self is required. Plants that fall into this category originate in cold climates and are naturally adept at coping with cold, winds and frosts.

As a novice gardener I tended to grow plants that were considered fully hardy, having neither the time nor space to nurture more tender species. (That said, if you have the luxury of space that can act as winter shelter, whether a porch, polytunnel, conservatory or greenhouse, don't be put off growing some of the less hardy species.)

Frost hardy: hardy to -5°C/23°F

Plants in this category can withstand temperatures as low as -5°C/23°F. Once temperatures dip below this, especially for any length of time, the plant may suffer lasting harm or even death. The plants need their roots protected from being frozen, and their top-growth from being terminally damaged by frosts. This is why you are advised to protect them with horticultural fleece (available from all garden centres) or provide shelter, such as a frost-free greenhouse.

Fleece can be packed around the base of a plant, to protect the roots, or wrapped around the plant itself and tied with garden twine, to provide protection for the leaves and stems. Mulch the crowns of vulnerable plants with dry leaves, fern fronds or straw, and wrap containers in bubblewrap or old sacking. The idea is to provide a winter layer, rather like a scarf, to take the brunt of the weather, so it can't affect the plant directly.

Borderline

Sometimes plants are referred to as being 'borderline' between two classifications, such as fully hardy and frost hardy. This means that they are teetering on the edge of a category and may be adversely affected by cold snaps. Even plants that are tough enough to have been labelled fully hardy can sometimes be affected by prolonged periods of bitterly cold weather in cold regions or exposed sites. If in doubt, provide cover.

However, more and more, I find that plants that are deemed frost hardy will survive a severe winter if I mulch the roots well in late autumn and place them against a warm, sheltered wall in the winter months, protecting them from the worst of cold winds, rain and frosts. This has sometimes meant an emergency marathon around the garden scraping snow from susceptible plants or providing emergency fleecing for those that had looked like they might survive, but under the onslaught of cruel weather, are beginning to look decidedly feeble. Occasionally I might lose one, but by taking a cutting earlier in the year or dividing the plant in spring, I have an insurance policy in case of a fatality. Eventually, experience will lead you to make the right decisions for your garden plants and you'll know when to take a risk – or not, as the case may be.

Half hardy: hardy to 0°C/32°F

Plants in this category will withstand temperature drops down to 0°C/32°F. They need protection with horticultural fleece and dry mulches, cloches and cold frames, or frost-free shelter, such as a porch, greenhouse or conservatory, where the temperature will never dip below the stated tolerance. This ensures that the plants' roots are protected from being frozen, or their top-growth being fatally damaged by snow or frosts.

Cloches and cold frames provide a microclimate for the plants sheltering under them, giving protection from ice, wind, snow and excessive wet. In spring, when the weather warms up, they also act as a mini-greenhouse, allowing plants to come on faster than those planted in open ground. Be aware that the use of these has to be carefully judged: they have no frost thermostat, as in a greenhouse, and tender plants can be damaged.

Frost tender: not hardy below 5°C/41°F

Frost tender plants are those that are grown as annuals or that will not survive the severe winters of the British Isles without protection. Although you can protect a frost-tender plant from frosts, you will never make it hardy. The frost-tender rating will vary from plant to plant and is normally specified, but all perennial frost-tender plants must be overwintered in fleece, cloches or cold frames, or kept in a warm greenhouse or conservatory and moved outside, once all risks of frost have gone. Many of these plants will need a period of 'hardening off' (see page 118) before they can be moved outside from their protected environment. If a plant is moved straight outdoors from a warm place, the shock of the colder habitat may kill it. Hardening off is normally achieved

Fully hardy *Vitis coignetiae* displaying its autumn colours

over a period of up to six weeks, during which the plant's exposure to outdoor air temperatures and sunlight levels is gradually increased.

Drought tolerance

Plants need a supply of water to survive: there is no such thing as a plant that never needs water. So plants that are described as drought resistant or tolerant are those that can come through a prolonged period of low rainfall or water scarcity for some weeks without suffering lasting harm or death.

Many drought-tolerant plants are easily recognisable because they have silver-leaved foliage or slightly hairy or succulent leaves. In their countries of origin (on the shores of the Mediterranean, for example) they are accustomed to prolonged periods with little or no rainfall and they have adapted to cope with the dearth of water. In fact, their leaves aren't silver at all, but they are covered with a fine cuticle or membrane that prevents water loss and it is this film that gives them their characteristic glaucous-grey colouring.

Some plants simply aren't drought tolerant, and that includes many of those featured in this book. They tend to have lush, light green foliage that is more delicate than those of drought-tolerant species. Although they probably won't keel over and die if deprived of a week's watering, they are not tolerant of sustained drought conditions.

As climate conditions change, all gardeners are going to have to reconsider

Many climbers, including honeysuckle, are drought-tolerant too

their approach to gardening, so it is wise to implement some good old-fashioned plant husbandry to help plants survive lengthy periods of water scarcity. Here are some simple, practical suggestions.

- Apply garden mulches. This will help prevent water loss from the soil by trapping the moisture at the roots of the plant, where it can be taken up more effectively. Mulching can take place at any time of year as long as the ground is not dry or frozen; water the ground well first. It is by no means foolproof, but every little helps.
- Choose the right plant for the right place. Some plants are naturally more drought tolerant than others; if you have a sunny garden, ask the nursery or garden centre to suggest plants of Mediterranean origin.
- Water early in the morning or late at night (assuming you aren't suffering a hosepipe ban). This enables plants to absorb the maximum amount of water, ensuring it is not wasted by evaporation in the drying heat of the midday sun.
- Invest in water butts. These are widely available by mail order, online or from garden centres and will collect all the water from the house guttering. Having extra water reserves in water butts could mean the difference between a successful, if slightly diminished, summer garden or a bleached, burnt-to-a-crisp desert.

MULCHES

The term 'mulch' is used repeatedly in gardening books; it simply means spreading a thick layer of material on the soil or around the base of particular plants. There are many garden mulches to choose from. Some, such as home-made compost and well-rotted farmyard manure, have the benefit of injecting additional nutrients into the soil and improving its texture. Others, such as bark or wood chippings and recycled cocoa shells, will help retain moisture and suppress weeds, and also look attractive, but do not provide nutrients.

Problems

If you are an inexperienced gardener, it is easy to imagine you'll be spending all your spare time tending to sickening plants. Don't take too much notice. By and large, climbers are an easy group of plants to grow and are no more susceptible to pests and diseases than any other garden flowers, shrubs or trees. There is not a plant in the kingdom that won't suffer from some minor irritant, pest or disease in its lifetime. Rather like us, they are prone to common weaknesses and it is natural that some will fall prey to ill health at one time or another, but if you follow some pretty basic commonsense guidelines, you can't go wrong.

- Always buy healthy, vigorous plants in the first instance. A well cared for plant bought from a reputable source will naturally have a stronger resistance to disease.
- Ensure sufficient air circulation around and through your climbers. This is achieved with a little judicious pruning and will diminish the chances of plants falling foul of fungal diseases such as powdery mildew.
- Look after your soil. Healthy growth depends on a healthy soil; the better the soil, the easier it is for the plant to thrive. The cornerstone of any good gardening or organic practice is to feed the soil rather than the plant: this will result in stronger growth and better resistance to pests and diseases.
- Encourage the natural enemies of garden pests. Naturally occurring predators such as birds, frogs, toads, shrews, hedgehogs, ladybirds and predatory ground beetles will all reduce the amount of pest infestation and help to maintain a healthy garden environment.
- Adopt organic garden practices. These are better for your garden and the planet as well as being cheaper than chemical alternatives.

- Last, but by no means least, be vigilant. There is no substitute for this. If you keep a close eye on your plants, you will inevitably see problems before they race out of control. Aphids can soon smother plants but, if caught early, a mass infestation can be prevented. Similarly with leaf diseases, an early diagnosis can prevent more serious problems later.

It is well worth remembering that even the most talented, famous gardeners all have to deal with pests and diseases on a daily basis and you will very quickly learn the remedial action to take.

Leaf and stem pests

It is often an easier job to identify pests than plant diseases. Sometimes there are obvious signs, such as large, unsightly, chewed leaf edges, or you might catch a snail or slug red-handed! But quite often the culprit is nowhere in sight, so you have to look carefully at the evidence and then determine how best to deal with the problem. Here are some of the commonest garden leaf pests you will encounter and how you should deal with the little blighters. Rule one: Know your enemy…

Aphids include pests such as blackfly, greenfly and whitefly. They are hard to eradicate completely because they occur in large numbers, never in isolation. They are all sapsuckers feeding on the sap of young shoots, which causes the leaves and stems of a plant to curl and distort, and damages new emerging growth. This weakens the plant considerably. Aphids also excrete a sticky sugary substance, which is fed on by ants, so if you notice a large column of ants steadily advancing up the stems of your climbing roses, you have almost certainly got an aphid infestation.

Clematis suffering from aphid infestation

Whether you have blackfly, greenfly or whitefly, the symptoms and remedies are much the same for all of them. They are immediately recognisable, being about 3mm/⅛in long, with transparent greenish, black or whitish bodies. They normally form a seething mass camouflaging the young stems of roses or other affected plants, where the growth is young and sappy and easier to attack. Greenfly occur almost everywhere outdoors and affect just about every plant you can think of. Whitefly are more common indoors, in greenhouses and conservatories, and blackfly tend to favour elder and broad beans.
Solution Spray as often as needed with a few drops of washing-up liquid mixed with water. Alternatively, use a proprietary pest spray.

Brown scale *see* Scale insects, below

Caterpillars love eating the leaves of many plants, and the unsightly notching can spoil a good display.
Solution Pick off by hand or remove the leaves, complete with caterpillar residents still on board, and dispose of them. If the infestation is large, use a proprietary insecticide.

Earwigs are particularly fond of clematis and tend to nibble the young leaves and flowers. As they come out mainly at night, it is hard to prevent them inflicting damage unless you are prepared to stake out the garden at midnight with a proprietary pest spray.
Solution The damage is marginally unsightly, but is not worth getting too concerned about. The large amount of leaf growth generated throughout the growing season will invariably disguise the odd chewed leaf.

Froghoppers are responsible for the common white spit-like froth seen on the stems and leaves of garden plants in early summer and often called cuckoo spit. A small, green sap-sucking nymph is camouflaged inside this foam and this can stunt and distort plant growth. In truth, however, they are unlikely to cause serious damage.
Solution The damage is hardly worth bothering about. If it really concerns you, wash the froth off with soft-soap solution.

Leaf miners are the larvae of beetles, moths and flies. The name describes the damage they inflict on a plant quite graphically: they literally mine through the leaves. An infestation can be easily identified from the tell-tale brown and white tunnel patterns on the leaf surface.
Solution Pick off the affected leaves and dispose of them. If you have the luxury of

a garden bonfire, better still, burn them. You could also spray the leaves with a recommended product, carefully following the instructions.

Mealybug are most prevalent on houseplants, or indeed anything grown in a pot in a greenhouse or conservatory. They are tiny pinkish-grey sap-suckers and are easily recognisable as they are normally covered in a woolly coating. This is actually a wax layer, which acts as protective armour and makes it difficult to eradicate them.
Solution A couple of drops of washing-up liquid mixed with water and sprayed on the plant helps penetrate this layer (you can spray as often as you like until you are rid of the infestation as it does the plant no harm).

Red spider mite take many forms, but the most common is a sap-feeding mite which is prevalent on houseplants or anything grown in a pot in a greenhouse or conservatory. It is microscopic in size, which makes it hard to spot. However, if you notice mottled leaves or sudden yellowing for no fathomable reason and also note the presence of silky webs around the young leaves and tips of your plants, the chances are you have red spider mite.
Solution Spraying the underside of the leaves with an up-turned hose from the start of the growing period seems to prevent their colonisation. In a greenhouse, keep the humidity levels high by hosing it down inside once a day.

Biological controls are successful as long as they are introduced early enough in the growing season. *Phytoseiulus persimilis* is a predatory mite that reproduces much faster than red spider mite and will prey aggressively on the eggs, young and adult red spider mite themselves. They can be introduced into the greenhouse or conservatory, where the minimum constant temperature should be 16°C/61°F to ensure this treatment is reliably effective.

Red spider mite are very resistant to chemical sprays; you would have to apply a treatment three times a day at weekly intervals to get rid of them, which is a pretty heavy workload for the average gardener.

Scale insects' tiny shells or scales are found on stems and, more commonly, on the undersides of plant leaves. Their infestation may result in very poor growth in the plant. Keep a watchful eye, as large infestations can be hard to treat. Brown scale are small (3–6mm/¼in long) sapsuckers that affect cotoneaster and ceanothus (as well as peaches and indoor vines). They suck sap from the underside of leaves and appear as brown scales on the stems of plants. Often tell-tale black dusty patches will be spotted in affected plants, as the insects excrete a sticky substance called honeydew that attracts this sooty mould.
Solution A small attack is of negligible consequence, but a heavy infestation can be very damaging to a plant. Methylated spirit can be applied to the leaves using cotton wool or a cotton bud, or use a proprietary organic or chemical spray, available from the garden centre.

Slugs and snails are the two most common culprits for inflicting non-stop plant damage. Their appetite for leaf and flower material is legendary and they are such a common foe to the gardener that remedies for dealing with them are infamously numerous and vary greatly in their effectiveness. Look for slime trails and leaf damage: leaves that are munched close to the bottom of the plant are more likely to have been attacked by slugs; top leaf damage is more commonly inflicted by snails, who don't mind the climb!

Solution The slug pub is a small plastic tray which, when filled with beer and placed shallowly in the soil at the foot of the climber, attracts slugs and snails as effectively as the local drunk at Happy Hour! The slugs and snails are lured by the sugary liquid and drown before they even begin their ascent up the plant. Ah well, at least they die happy. There are also biological controls such as nematodes, which act in the same way as the nematodes described below. Alternatively, sprinkle slug pellets sparingly around the base of your plants. These will kill the slugs or snails on contact.

Thrips are more commonly known as thunderflies. They are black insects up to 2mm/¹⁄₁₆in long and feed on the leaf surface, leaving silvery patches and black dottings. They can also feed on flower petals, leaving much the same markings.
Solution In the greenhouse, try to keep the temperature cooler with plenty of ventilation, or hose the greenhouse floor with water in the mornings. Alternatively, treat with an insecticide available from garden centres.

Tortrix moth Caterpillars of the carnation moth affect many ornamental plants, binding themselves in the leaves, which are rolled up by silky threads to protect the caterpillar inside.
Solution Remove the affected leaves, complete with resident caterpillar, and dispose of them. Pheromone traps are available at garden centres or by mail order, or treat the exposed caterpillar with insecticide.

Vine weevil most commonly affect plants grown in containers and pots, although they can also damage plants growing in open ground. The adult beetle is easily recognised by its long pointed snout; it feeds voraciously on the foliage of herbaceous plants and shrubs, causing unsightly notching along the edges of the leaves. This might be unattractive, but rarely proves fatal to the plant. The real damage is done by their ghastly offspring: the larvae are hatched at the roots of the plants the parents are feeding on and the infants' diet is the plant's roots.

The first noticeable sign of the larvae being present may be a yellowing of the leaves, poor growth and a wilting plant that does not respond to watering. More often there is very little warning and it is not uncommon to see an otherwise healthy plant suddenly keel over before you have even realised you have an infestation.
Solution There is a nematode available: this is a form of microscopic parasitic eelworm that enters the larvae and releases bacteria that kill the grubs. To add to their effectiveness, the nematodes keep reproducing inside the dead grub.

Alternatively, a chemical drench can be watered over pots. This will kill the larvae and is available from garden centres.

Woolly aphids can affect cotoneaster and pyracantha (as well as apples, pears and cherries). The aphids are protected inside white cotton-wool like growths, which appear particularly around old pruning points. Lumps may appear under the stem bark, leaving the plant vulnerable to canker.
Solution If the infestation is minor, paint with methylated spirit and scrape them off, or scrub them with a hard brush and warm soapy water. Alternatively, chemical applications are available from garden centres.

Plant diseases

Plant diseases can be a lot harder to spot than something as obvious as a snail attack. Like human beings, plants are prone to infections and diseases, but it is not always easy to recognise that a plant is sickly, let alone find the cause of the trouble, and prevention is better than cure. Here are a few tips for keeping your plants disease free.

- Grow disease-resistant varieties wherever possible.
- Plant the right plant in the right place: a shade-loving plant will struggle in a warm, sunny position and will be more vulnerable to infection.
- Keep plants well watered and mulched to prevent roots from drying out. By caring for your plants with regular watering and feeding, you are equipping them with a stronger resistance to disease.
- Improve the airflow round the plants by avoiding planting them too closely together and pruning out congested stems in the centre of the plant.

LEFT TO RIGHT Blackspot, mildew and rust

- Practise good hygiene in the greenhouse and in the garden: this is an obvious deterrent to plant sickness. Clear up dead or damaged leaves in the garden, always make sure pots are washed and clean before potting up new plants or seedlings, and generally keep things shipshape.

However, you are likely to meet one or two nasty diseases at some point, no matter how hard you try to prevent it, so here are some of the more common plant diseases you will come across, and their remedies.

Blackspot is a fungal disease which affects roses and is most commonly seen during prolonged bouts of wet weather, as it is typically spread by water splashes and rain. Black markings appear on leaves, which then drop off prematurely. Many new roses have been bred with an in-built resistance to blackspot, so it is well worth pursuing any of these.

Solution Remove all infected foliage and dispose of it, so that you are not spreading the disease by leaving infected material lying around. Spraying skimmed milk mixed with water at regular two-weekly intervals will keep the problem in check fairly effectively.

If you prefer, spray with a recommended chemical control.

Clematis wilt is a fungal disease that has some gardeners gasping with terror, but although the symptoms are severe, it need not prove terminal. Wilt normally occurs on clematis that is just about to break into flower. The leaves turn grey, a certain portion of the climber may appear to have dried to a crisp or, worse still, the whole plant collapses unexpectedly.
Solution Remove and destroy all infected growth as it appears and give the plant a generous feed and thorough soaking. If caught early, this should lead to a good recovery. One of the best preventive measures is to plant the clematis deeply in the first place (see page 104).

Fireblight is a bacterial infection and is potentially very serious if not treated early. The first signs are flowers that blacken and wither. Once advanced, the leaves will yellow, then blacken; ultimately, weeping cankers will appear on woody stems or branches. It can affect cotoneaster.
Solution Prune out all infected branches or stems immediately, cutting back to healthy growth. Burn all the material and wash or disinfect the pruning saw thoroughly, so as not to infect other garden plants. If the plant is too far gone and on death's door, dig it up and burn it.

Powdery mildew is a common fungal disease that arises from meagre growing conditions and poor air circulation. It is easily recognisable as a white powdery substance on the leaves, which if left untreated will turn leaves brown and result in stunted or distorted growth.
Solution Remove all affected areas and improve air circulation. Try to water plants from the base, without wetting the leaves, as this prevents the disease spreading by water splashes. If annuals are affected, but have already had a good flowering period, pull up the entire plant and dispose of it. Proprietary fungicide sprays are available from garden centres, but it is as well to remember that prevention is always better than cure (see page 113).

Rose ball occurs during excessively wet weather, causing rose buds and blooms to brown on the stem, without ever opening.
Solution Remove spoiled flowers.

Root rot is a fungal disease that occurs when soil is wet or waterlogged. Roots literally rot in the soil, causing the death of the plant. It can affect actinidia, but is a rare occurrence.
Solution Keep an open, well-drained soil. Affected plants need to be dug up and destroyed.

Rust is another fungal disease, and is more likely to be seen in moist, damp conditions. It can be diagnosed by round coloured patches of orangey brown pustules developing on the undersides of leaves. Hollyhocks, iris and roses are all susceptible to rust.
Solution Good hygiene is the surest way to help prevent fungal diseases, but it can be hard to prevent the occurrence of rust, as it is most prevalent in extremely wet weather conditions. Prune the plants to improve air circulation and remove and burn all infected leaves. Ensure all affected leaves are also removed from the top of the soil before they decompose and spread the infection. If rust is left unchecked, the life of the plant is at risk.

Pruning

Pruning removes parts of a plant in order to promote flowering and to restrict its size and spread. Cutting away any large amount of plant material is referred to as 'hard pruning'; it normally stimulates the plant into putting out vigorous growth. Cutting out a moderate amount of growth from the plant is known as 'light pruning' and generates moderate new growth.

Pruning stimulates the plant to grow in a particular way. A good pruning regime will encourage health and vigour, enhance ornamental displays in many species, and regulate the height and shape of a plant. Because pruning involves making numerous cuts to the plant stems, it should always be done with a clean, sharp pair of secateurs to minimise damage to the plant. And always cut back to healthy buds, but don't make the cut so close as to damage those developing buds.

Deadheading is the simplest form of pruning. It simply means cutting off the spent flowers. It encourages new flower buds to burst forth in repeating rose types, or will assist continuous flowerers to keep putting out their blooms. It also keeps the plant looking tidy and will help prevent diseases setting in. Roses that produce ornamental hips (mainly species and shrub roses) should not be deadheaded, and it is not worth deadheading late-flowering clematis, as they produce such ornamental seed heads after they flower.

One of the main objectives of pruning is to develop or train your plant into an attractive, uncongested, open framework of stems that will maximise any flowering display or show foliage to its best advantage. For any climber, the aim in the first two or three years of formative pruning is to build a strong framework of branching stems.

TOOLS

The right tools for the job make any task 100 per cent easier. You will need:

- a good-quality pair of anvilled secateurs (this is essential – the kitchen scissors or an old garden knife are not going to do you or your plants any favours)
- a strong pair of loppers for the more vigorous plants, such as climbing and rambling roses, whose stems get very thick and woody
- a good-quality pair of gardening gloves to protect your hands
- garden twine to hand, in an apron or pocket, for tying in stems

Pruning an early-flowering clematis

After planting, tie the main stem into the support. In the first spring of the plant's growth, choose strong shoots to create a basic framework, and encourage those young stems or tendrils by helping them attach to the point where they are needed, gently tying them in with garden twine.

Once the risk of severe frost has passed in the following spring, cut back each side shoot to a point just above a bud near the main stem and again secure the newly pruned shoots to their supports. Several strong shoots will grow from each of these stems during the following season; these, again, will be used to form the plant's framework. Tie them in to the support as they develop.

In the third spring, cut back each stem to a bud that is pointing in the direction in which the stem is to be trained to ensure that the shoots branch out and create better coverage. Tie in all the stems with soft twine and cut back other new shoots to within two buds of the nearest stem.

Additionally, as the plant matures, prune out old or congested plant material. This effectively increases the air circulation around a plant, which is very beneficial in the prevention of pests and diseases. It also balances the growth of the plant, preventing it getting straggly, top heavy or turning into a congested, tangled mess.

Take time with the early formative pruning, as it will pay dividends later on and help keep the plant under control, as well as maximising its flowering or fruiting potential. How and when to prune varies according to the plant; more detailed information on training particular climbers on to a framework of wires or other supports will be found in the sections for clematis (page 60), roses (page 40) and wisteria (page 24).

Propagation

Propagating climbers is, by and large, an easy process, and there are all kinds of reasons for having a go at it. Perhaps you want to share a favourite plant with a friend, or raise a number of plants for a plant sale; if you have a large garden, buying the quantity you require from the garden centre may just be too expensive, and growing plants from cuttings or seeds might be the only affordable route. Multiplying plants by propagation is a cost-effective method of increasing their numbers and a hugely enjoyable and satisfying occupation too.

Most perennial climbers are propagated from cuttings or by layering, and both these methods are easy and reliable, even for the novice gardener. The absolutely marvellous thing about propagating plants in this way is that the process will produce new plants that are identical to the parent plant from which the cutting material was taken. These are known as clones, and they will exhibit all the characteristics of the original plant.

Annual climbers or tender perennials have to be raised yearly, usually from seed. Growing plants from seed is cheap, though not always entirely reliable: some seeds germinate more easily than others, and whilst seed from some species will grow to resemble, more or less, the plant that you collected the seed from, seed from hybrids will almost certainly produce a very different plant from the parent. Bought seed can be expected to grow true.

Bear in mind that if you have never attempted propagation of any kind, your first results may not always be brilliant and you might have more luck with one plant than another. Because all plants mature according to different seasons, all seed sowing and cuttings are greatly affected by changes in weather and temperature: poor timing can mean the difference between success and failure. But like anything in life, a little practice and know-how will lead to success. Don't be put off by what seems a complicated process: it is a lot simpler in practice than the description of the procedure!

Growing climbers from seed

Many of the leading seed merchants have a huge variety of annual climbers to choose from, including the cup and saucer vine (*Cobaea scandens*), clematis and so many more. If you want to be sure of growing a particular plant, it is best to buy the seed, as plants grown from collected seed can be variable. However, provided you have the space (a windowsill will do), growing from seed is generally easy and you can widen the repertoire and choice of your garden plants immensely by growing the odd annual or two. They are easy to care for, too, and as they are only growing for one season, you have no worries about training or pruning.

Many perennial seeds, as well as hardy tree and shrub seeds, require special treatment before planting to ensure germination will occur. There are a great many processes – from heat-treatments, soaking seed to scarification – but most are carried out by seed suppliers nowadays, so you rarely have to worry about them.

Cold stratification mimics the naturally occurring seasonal changes that lead to seed germination, and can be achieved by planting seed in a pot of compost and leaving them outside for between three to eight weeks. Germination (the emergence of a shoot from the seed case) should occur readily and the seeds can then be grown on in pots of prepared compost. Alternatively, place seed in a polythene bag and leave in

the fridge. Check at regular intervals, remove any seeds that show signs of germination and plant them immediately in a prepared pot of compost. Label it clearly.

Annual climbers are best grown in pots and then transplanted into their final positions, but you can sow some seeds, such as sweet peas and nasturtiums, directly outdoors into their final flowering positions.

Sowing

Sowing seeds is easy. Whether they are home-harvested or bought from seed suppliers, the sowing regime is the same. Seed packets are labelled with clear information on how and when to plant them, and all you need is clean pots or seed trays, fresh potting compost and either a greenhouse or warm windowsill.

1 Prepare your seed trays by filling them with a good potting compost to 6mm/¼in or so below the rim of the tray or pot, firm it down well and water lightly. A word of warning here – seedlings can be affected by a process known as 'damping off', whereby all your fresh little green seedlings can literally wilt and wither overnight. A light drenching of Cheshunt compound (available from garden centres) over your composted pots or trays prior to seed sowing should prevent this rather dismal malady.

2 Check your seed packet for exact instructions on how to sow particular seed. Some seeds will need to be covered with compost, whilst others can sit lightly on the surface. Larger seeds can be sown two or three to a pot. Label each tray or pot clearly and water lightly again. This is best done with a mister or with a watering can with a 'rose' spout to avoid washing the seed into puddles.

3 Place the seed trays or pots on a light, non-draughty windowsill, in a sheltered porch or in a greenhouse. (Heated propagators are inexpensive to buy and will give newly sown

seeds the optimum soil temperature for germination. I can heartily recommend them to novice growers, as they are sure to give more reliable results.)

4 Water regularly, keeping the compost moist, but not wet. Within a few weeks, seedlings will appear and you can begin to open the vents on your propagator to regulate the air temperature as they grow.

Eventually there comes a time to 'thin out' your seedlings. This means weeding out the weaker-looking ones, allowing the stronger, larger ones more space to grow. This can be done in the seed tray, leaving a limited number of plants growing away, but inevitably a seed tray is not going to be deep enough to accommodate a burgeoning new plant. The alternative is to transfer the maturing seedlings into individual pots, a process known as 'pricking out'. The route you choose will depend on how many plants you need and what space you have available for growing.

HARDENING OFF

Plants grown in protected, indoor conditions cannot be put straight into the ground outdoors without a period of 'hardening off'. This is a method of gradually acclimatising your rather spoilt, pampered plants to colder outdoor conditions over a period of weeks. Once all danger of frosts has passed, simply expose the new plants to outdoor conditions. If you have the luxury of a greenhouse, open the vents for a couple of hours to allow colder air to circulate, gradually increasing the length of time the vents are open during the day, and closing them at night; or leave them in a cold frame that is left open in the daytime and then closed at night. If you are growing on a windowsill, leave the window open for a few hours each day to help them adapt to outdoor temperatures. After two to six weeks they should be sufficiently tough to brave it outdoors permanently in the places they are to flower.

Direct all your love and attention to the remainder of your seedlings by watering regularly until such time as you have fully fledged new plants ready to face the outside world.

Growing climbers from cuttings

A cutting is a small piece cut from the stem or root of an existing plant and grown on in a separate pot to produce a new plant, exactly like the one it was taken from. Most climbers are propagated from cuttings. There are different types of cutting: most commonly, 'nodal' or 'internodal' cuttings, semi-ripe, heel or root cuttings. Softwood cuttings, which are taken in early summer from fresh 'soft' growth, have the highest rate of success, and hardwood cuttings are taken in winter from hardened, sturdier growth. Layering is also an excellent way of producing new plants, especially for many of the clematis.

Growing new plants from cuttings is not difficult. Here's a list of the equipment you will need, and its preparation: hygiene is an important factor when taking cuttings, and these simple practices will all help successful propagation.

- A clean, sharp garden knife or penknife: sterilise it by holding it over a small flame (and then let it cool before using it!)
- Fresh potting compost: never use old compost that has been lying around or has been used for growing other plants
- Clean pots: if you are re-using old pots, give them a thorough scrub with warm soapy water, rinse and allow to dry
- A watering can with a fine 'rose' spout, full of water
- Hormone rooting powder (optional)
- Clean, clear plastic bags

LEFT TO RIGHT A softwood cutting, lower leaves removed; semi-ripe cuttings, ready for preparation; preparing an internodal cutting

Choosing cutting material

The idea here is to remove a part of an existing plant in such a way that you can nip back to the potting shed and turn it into a cutting. This will grow into a new plant.

- Always choose cutting material from a healthy, vigorous plant: a cutting taken from a weak, sickly plant will not do well.
- Avoid any shoots affected by pests, disease or damage.
- Take cutting material that is young and juvenile and look for strong, non-flowering sideshoots, taking them from different areas of the plant and avoiding those at the base. (If you take all your cuttings from one area of the plant, you will leave the original plant looking hacked to death and lopsided.)
- Place cutting material in a sealed plastic bag and keep in a cool place until you are ready to prepare the cutting and pot it up: this will help to prevent water loss, but cuttings need to be potted up almost immediately, whilst still fresh. They are of no use once they have wilted.

My experience is that cuttings root more successfully when taken in the morning, when plants are full of water. This makes sense because, once detached from the parent plant, the cutting material loses its ability to feed itself from roots or any other means.

Softwood cuttings

Softwood cuttings are taken from a young sideshoot, just below a leaf joint or node, when there is fresh, new growth on the plant. They have a high rooting success rate but, because the growth is young and tender, they are susceptible to bruising and need to be handled delicately. They are prone to wilting, so speed is of the essence.

1 Choose a healthy stem, cut a section of it away cleanly from the original plant and then make a further clean cut in that section, just below a node or leaf joint. The final cutting should be about 5cm/2in long and have two or three pairs of leaves.
2 Prepare your pots with a good-quality potting compost and ensure the soil is firmed down well, using your fingertips. It is also beneficial to apply a light drench of antifungal solution, such as Cheshunt compound, to help prevent fungal disease, as young cuttings are very susceptible.
3 Holding the cutting gently by the leaves, so as not to damage the stem, dip the cut end lightly into hormone rooting powder, tapping off any excess powder. This step is optional, but it can help accelerate rooting.

4 Using a dibber, or your fingertip, make a small hole in the surface of the compost. Still holding the cutting by the leaves, insert the cutting into the hole and firm the soil gently around the base of the stem. This will ensure it makes good contact with the compost and will prevent air pockets.

5 Water well, using a fine spray, label the pot and sit back and wait for the new plantlet to form roots. This should take about three to four weeks, or perhaps less in a heated propagator providing bottom heat. Never let the pot dry out, but equally don't over-water, leaving the cutting sitting in sodden compost, as this may cause it to rot.

Climbers that can be propagated by softwood cuttings include bougainvillea, ceanothus, celastrus, euonymus, honeysuckle (*Lonicera*), ivy (*Hedera*), jasmine, Virginia creeper (*Parthenocissus*), passionflower (*Passiflora*), quince (*Chaenomeles*) and wisteria.

A nodal cutting is one taken immediately below a node or bud. An internodal cutting is taken from the stem, cutting between two nodes or buds. Whether you take nodal or internodal cuttings is entirely up to you and will have no detrimental effect on the growth of the cutting. Internodal cuttings are taken at the same time of year as nodal cuttings but have the advantage that a greater number of cuttings can be taken from each stem.

For internodal cuttings, make a clean cut between the nodes or leaf joints so you have a cutting approximately 10–15cm/4–6in in length. Carefully pinch out the lower leaves so you are left with a bare stem with a pair of leaves. If the leaves are large, cut them in half with a clean, sharp knife, to reduce water loss. Pot them up as described above. Planting cuttings is often referred to as

'striking' in gardening books, which is just a posh way of saying 'Pot 'em up!'.

Greenwood cuttings

These are taken from the shoot tips of a plant when the stems are still young and pliable, but not too fragile, and beginning to firm up somewhat. They are not as delicate in handling as softwood cuttings and less prone to wilt.

To take a greenwood cutting, identify a sideshoot or stem of firm but bendy growth. Detach it at the point where it joins the older plant growth. You will be left with a single main stem and several leaf shoots coming off it. Trim off the soft top shoots just above the node, leaving you with a cutting some 25cm/10in long with three leaf nodes. Trim any large remaining leaves to half their size with a sharp knife to prevent moisture loss from the cutting. Nick the base of the stem with a sharp knife and dip this end into hormone rooting powder, shake off any excess and insert each cutting into a suitable potting compost, deep enough that they stand upright. Water well and label.

Actinidia, cotoneaster, quince (*Chaenomeles*) and pyracantha are all suited to greenwood cuttings.

Semi-ripe cuttings

These are taken a little later in the growing season, usually between June and August, when the stems are still young but are beginning to get firmer and buds are present, therefore they aren't so easily bruised when handling.

Choose the current year's growth and cut a shoot that is firm at the base, but softer at the tip. Make a clean cut just below a node or leaf joint so you have a cutting approximately 10–15cm/4–6in in length. Carefully pinch out the lower leaves and the soft tip, leaving a bare stem with a pair of leaves. If the leaves are large, reduce their size by half, cutting with a clean, sharp knife, to minimise water loss.

Pot the cutting up as described above for softwood cuttings. Semi-ripe and heel cuttings are not so prone to fungal diseases as softwood cuttings, so newly potted plants can be placed in a cold frame or cool greenhouse.

Jasmine, honeysuckle (*Lonicera*) and Virginia creeper (*Parthenocissus*) are all suitable for semi-ripe cuttings.

Heel cuttings

Heel cuttings are an excellent way of propagating plants that are a bit tricky by other methods. They are normally taken from late July to September, as for semi-ripe cuttings. Select short side shoots and peel them carefully away from the stem, so that a sliver or heel of the old woody stem is still attached. This will contain hormones that will help speed up the rooting process. Pot them up in exactly the same way as semi-ripe cuttings. Cotoneaster, winter jasmine and honeysuckle (*Lonicera*) can all be done this way.

Taking a heel cutting

Root cuttings

These are taken from vigorous, young roots of a plant and are normally used for plants that naturally produce suckers or shoots from the root area. These are taken from healthy roots when the plant is dormant.

Choose a root about 10cm/4in long and about as thick as a pencil. Make cuts along the length of the root – straight one end, angled the other – depending on how many cuttings you require, so that each is approximately 4cm/1½in long. Wash off the soil, pat dry and dust the cuttings with a fungicide (available from garden centres). Insert each cutting into the soil of a prepared pot of compost so that the flat ends are just visible above the surface. Cover with a thin layer of sharp sand, water and label.

Leaf-bud cuttings

A leaf-bud cutting consists of a leaf attached to a short section of stem with a healthy bud in the joint between the leaf and the stem. You will normally get only one cutting per stem.

Root cuttings ready for insertion

Layering a climbing hydrangea, the trailing stem weighted down with a stone

Simple layering

This is the easiest method for propagating a huge variety of climbers. It is foolproof and almost always successful. Simply select a healthy trailing stem from the parent plant that is lying on the soil. Either simply weight it down with a stone, or bury a plastic garden pot, filled with a good standard potting compost, into the soil. Peg the selected stem down over the top of the pot, cover lightly with compost so that it is firmly anchored into the soil, insert a bamboo cane, label it clearly, water regularly and wait. Check a few months later and you will invariably find that this section of the stem will have produced roots and new shoots. Detach it from the parent plant, lift the pot if used, water it well, label it and, hey presto – you have a new plant!

Many plants, such as actinidia, akebia, campsis, celastrus, climbing hydrangea, fig (*Ficus*), golden hop (*Humulus lupulus* 'Aureus'), honeysuckle (*Lonicera*), ivy (*Hedera*), jasmine, pileostegia, some solanums and wisteria will naturally self-layer or are suitable for the simple layering method.

The gardening year

Gardens can be high maintenance or low maintenance – but there is no such thing as a no-maintenance garden! First and foremost, be realistic about how much time you can afford to spend in the garden. Typically, you will have to water, weed, feed and attend to your plants' needs. Some times of year are busier than others, but there is no point growing plants that need masses of your time if you have to be a weekend gardener.

Spring

Spring is always busy. This is a good time to get new plants established and to start mulching and seed sowing. Most plants will appreciate feeding at the onset of the growing season. You can use organic mulches for ground plants (see page 108) or slow-release fertilisers for plants grown in pots.

Spring is also the time for many climbers to be cut back or pruned, and for stray growth that may have been damaged by strong winds during the winter to be cut out or tied in. This could take very little time in a courtyard setting, or days in a large acreage.

As the growing season starts, weeds begin their relentless march. Weeding is a necessary chore. Try to do it little but often, so you aren't confronted with a large infestation. If you are growing your climbers in containers, pulling out the odd weed is hardly strenuous. In a border, take a little time to prevent weeds establishing themselves at the base of the assorted plants or climbers.

Summer

Summer is an easy time, when you can enjoy your garden with most of the hard work behind you. Keeping up with watering regimes, weeding, deadheading and securing vigorous new growth is the most you will have to contend with. Pots and containers may need to be watered up to twice a day, especially in dry periods. Depending on your soil and whether or not you mulch your beds, as well as the weather conditions, flower borders will need watering at least three times a week, sometimes more.

Autumn

Autumn is a time to tidy. Clear up old leaves and garden debris to help promote a healthy, hygienic garden environment and to prevent disease from overwintering in decaying matter. Most deciduous climbers respond well to autumn pruning. This is another good time to plant, but don't leave it too late in the year, as planting when the soil is warm will help new plant roots establish more quickly.

Winter

For most gardeners, winter brings a well-earned rest. Put your feet up with a cup of tea and a seed catalogue and plan the garden for next year. If it's not too nippy, inspect the garden for dead, diseased and damaged plants. Wash out all your garden pots with warm soapy water and a stiff brush, and give the greenhouse (if you have one) a good hosing down both inside and out.

As the days lengthen, but the weather is perhaps still a little brisk for sitting out, make yourself useful by getting a head start on the weeding and applying garden mulches to your flower beds and plants. Then you can look forward to the start of another gardening year.

Time to enjoy: a summer garden in full bloom

Climbers for specific purposes

When you choose a climber, see how many boxes you can get it to tick, in terms of flower, foliage, perfume, berries or seed heads. If you can tick two or three of these categories, you can be sure you have chosen a climber that will bring seasonal interest and charm to your garden spaces.

Fragrance

Actinidia deliciosa
A. kolomikta
Akebia quinata
Araujia sericifera
Billardiera longiflora
Chaenomeles speciosa
  'Geisha Girl'
C. s. 'Moerloosei'
Chimonanthus praecox
  'Luteus'
Clematis 'Apple Blossom'
C. armandii
C. cirrhosa var. balearica
C. c. var. purpurascens
  'Freckles'
C. 'Elizabeth'
C. flammula
C. montana var. rubens
  'Odorata'
C. m. var. r. 'Pink Perfection'
C. m. var. r. 'Tetrarose'
C. 'Rosea'
C. x triternata
  'Rubromarginata'
C. vitalba
Cobaea scandens
Hoya carnosa
Humulus lupulus 'Aureus'
Jasminum beesianum
J. nudiflorum
J. officinale
J. o. 'Clotted Cream'
J. o. Fiona Sunrise (also
  known as 'Frojas')
J. polyanthum
J. x stephanense
Lathyrus odoratus
Lonicera x brownii
  'Dropmore Scarlet'
L. x italica
L. japonica
L. j. 'Halliana'
L. periclymenum 'Belgica'
L. p. 'Serotina'
L. x purpusii 'Winter Beauty'
Pileostegia viburnoides
Rosa 'Albéric Barbier'

R. 'Albertine'
R. Altissimo (also known as
  'Delmur')
R. 'American Pillar'
R. banksiae 'Lutea'
R. 'Bantry Bay'
R. 'Climbing Cécile Brünner'
R. 'Climbing Iceberg'
R. 'Constance Spry'
R. 'Crimson Glory Climbing'
R. 'Danse du Feu'
R. filipes 'Kiftsgate'
R. 'Gloire de Dijon'
R. 'Golden Showers'
R. 'New Dawn'
R. 'Rambling Rector'
R. 'Zéphirine Drouhin'
Schisandra rubriflora
Schizophragma hydrangeoides
  'Roseum'
Solanum crispum
S. laxum 'Album' (formerly S.
  jasminoides 'Album')
Stauntonia hexaphylla
Stephanotis floribunda
Trachelospermum jasminoides
Vitis coignetiae
Wisteria floribunda 'Multijuga'
  (formerly 'Macrobotrys')
W. f. 'Rosea'
W. sinensis
W. s. 'Alba'

Containers

Abutilon megapotamicum
Ampelopsis brevipedunculata
  var. maximowiczii 'Elegans'
Araujia sericifera
Asteranthera ovata
Berberidopsis corallina
Billardiera longiflora
Bougainvillea x buttiana 'Mrs
  Butt'
Calystegia hederacea 'Flore
  Pleno'
Ceanothus 'Italian Skies'
Chimonanthus praecox
  'Luteus'

Clematis 'Apple Blossom'
C. 'Bill MacKenzie'
C. cirrhosa var. balearica
C. c. var. purpurascens
  'Freckles'
C. c. 'Wisley Cream'
C. 'Continuity'
C. x durandii
C. 'Frances Rivis'
C. 'Gipsy Queen'
C. 'Helsingborg'
C. napaulensis
C. 'Nelly Moser'
C. 'Princess Diana'
C. 'Purple Spider'
C. 'Rosea'
C. 'Royal Velours'
C. tibetana subsp. vernayi
  'Glasnevin Dusk'
C. 'Venosa Violacea'
Clianthus puniceus
Cobaea scandens
Cotoneaster frigidus
  'Cornubia'
C. horizontalis
C. lacteus
Eccremocarpus scaber
Euonymus fortunei 'Emerald
  'n' Gold'
E. f. 'Silver Queen'
x Fatshedera lizei
Ficus pumila
Fremontodendron 'California
  Glory'
Hardenbergia violacea
Hedera algeriensis 'Gloire de
  Marengo' (formerly H.
  canariensis)
H. helix 'Buttercup'
H. h. 'Parsley Crested'
  (formerly 'Cristata')
H. h. 'Pedata'
Hoya carnosa
Humulus lupulus 'Aureus'
Ipomoea tricolor 'Heavenly
  Blue'
Jasminum beesianum
J. mesnyi

J. nudiflorum
J. officinale 'Clotted Cream'
J. o. Fiona Sunrise (also
  known as 'Frojas')
J. polyanthum
Lapageria rosea
Lathyrus latifolius
L. odoratus
Lonicera x purpusii 'Winter
  Beauty'
Plumbago auriculata
Pyracantha rogersiana
P. Saphyr Orange (also
  known as 'Cadange')
Rosa Altissimo (also known
  as 'Delmur')
R. 'Bantry Bay'
R. 'Climbing Cécile
  Brünner'
R. 'Climbing Iceberg'
R. 'Constance Spry'
R. 'Danse du Feu'
R. 'Golden Showers'
R. 'New Dawn'
R. Warm Welcome (also
  known as 'Chewizz')
R. 'Zéphirine Drouhin'
Schizophragma hydrangeoides
  'Roseum'
Sollya heterophylla
Stephanotis floribunda
Thunbergia alata
Tropaeolum majus 'African
  Queen'

Full sun
All except:
Asteranthera ovata
Berberidopsis corallina
Humulus lupulus 'Aureus'
Lapageria rosea
Lonicera periclymenum
  'Serotina'

Full shade
Cotoneaster lacteus
Hedera colchica 'Dentata
  Variegata'

H. c. 'Sulphur Heart'
(formerly 'Paddy's Pride')
H. helix
H. h. 'Parsley Crested'
(formerly 'Cristata')
H. h. 'Pedata'
H. hibernica
Holboellia coriacea
Lapageria rosea
Parthenocissus henryana
P. quinquefolia
P. tricuspidata 'Veitchii'
Pileostegia viburnoides

Partial shade

*Denotes plants that have
significantly reduced
flowering in shaded
position
Abutilon megapotamicum
Akebia quinata
A. trifoliata
Ampelopsis brevipedunculata
var. maximowiczii
'Elegans'*
Araujia sericifera
Aristolochia macrophylla
(formerly A. durior)
Asteranthera ovata
Berberidopsis corallina
Billardiera longiflora
Celastrus orbiculatus
C. scandens
Chaenomeles speciosa
'Geisha Girl'
C. s. 'Moerloosei'
Clematis 'Bill MacKenzie'*
C. cirrhosa var. balearica
C. 'Continuity'
C. × durandii
C. 'Elizabeth'*
C. flammula
C. 'Frances Rivis'
C. 'Gipsy Queen'*
C. 'Helsingborg'
C. 'M. Koster' (formerly
'Margot Koster')*
C. montana var. grandiflora *
C. m. var. rubens 'Odorata'*
C. m. var. r. 'Pink Perfection'*
C. m. var. r. 'Tetrarose'*
C. 'Nelly Moser'
C. 'Princess Diana'*
C. 'Purple Spider'*
C. 'Rosea'
C. 'Royal Velours'*
C. tangutica*
C. tibetana subsp. vernayi
'Glasnevin Dusk'*

C. × triternata
'Rubromarginata'*
C. 'Venosa Violacea'*
C. vitalba
Cotoneaster frigidus
'Cornubia'
C. horizontalis
C. lacteus
Euonymus fortunei 'Emerald
'n' Gold'
E. f. 'Silver Queen'
× Fatshedera lizei
Ficus pumila
Garrya elliptica 'James Roof'
Hardenbergia violacea*
Hedera algeriensis 'Gloire de
Marengo' (formerly H.
canariensis)
H. colchica 'Dentata'
H. c. 'Dentata Variegata'
H. c. 'Sulphur Heart'
(formerly 'Paddy's Pride')
H. helix
H. h. 'Buttercup'*
H. h. 'Oro di Bogliasco'
(formerly 'Goldheart')
H. h. 'Parsley Crested'
(formerly 'Cristata')
H. h. 'Pedata'
H. hibernica
Holboellia coriacea
Hoya carnosa
Humulus lupulus 'Aureus'*
Hydrangea anomola subsp.
petiolaris
Jasminum mesnyi*
J. nudiflorum*
J. officinale
J. o. 'Clotted Cream'*
J. o. Fiona Sunrise (also
known as 'Frojas')*
J. × stephanense*
Lapageria rosea
Lathyrus latifolius*
L. odoratus*
Lonicera × brownii
'Dropmore Scarlet'
L. × italica
L. japonica
L. j. 'Halliana'
L. periclymenum 'Belgica'
L. p. 'Serotina'
L. × purpusii 'Winter Beauty'
Parthenocissus henryana
P. quinquefolia
P. tricuspidata 'Veitchii'
Passiflora caerulea*
Pileostegia viburnoides
Pyracantha rogersiana

P. Saphyr Orange (also
known as 'Cadange')
Rosa 'Albéric Barbier'
R. 'Albertine'
R. Altissimo (also known as
'Delmur')*
R. 'Bantry Bay'*
R. 'Constance Spry'*
R. 'Danse du Feu'
R. 'Gloire de Dijon'
R. 'New Dawn'*
R. Warm Welcome (also
known as 'Chewizz')*
R. 'Zéphirine Drouhin'*
Schisandra rubriflora
Schizophragma hydrangeoides
'Roseum'
Sollya heterophylla*
Stauntonia hexaphylla
Tropaeolum speciosum*
Vitis amurensis
V. vinifera 'Purpurea'
Wisteria floribunda 'Multijuga'
(formerly 'Macrobotrys')
W. f. 'Rosea'
W. sinensis
W. s. 'Alba'

North-facing walls

Ampelopsis brevipedunculata
var. maximowiczii 'Elegans'
Akebia quinata
A. trifoliata
Asteranthera ovata
Celastrus orbiculatus
Chaenomeles speciosa
'Geisha Girl'
C. s. 'Moerloosei'
Clematis 'Bill MacKenzie'
C. 'Continuity'
C. × durandii
C. 'Elizabeth'
C. 'Gipsy Queen'
C. 'Helsingborg'
C. 'M. Koster' (formerly
'Margot Koster')
C. montana var. grandiflora
C. m. var. rubens 'Odorata'
C. m. var. r. 'Pink Perfection'
C. m. var. r. 'Tetrarose'
C. 'Nelly Moser'
C. 'Purple Spider'
C. 'Rosea'
C. × triternata
'Rubromarginata'
C. 'Venosa Violacea'
Cotoneaster frigidus
'Cornubia'
C. lacteus

Euonymus fortunei 'Emerald
'n' Gold'
E. f. 'Silver Queen'
× Fatshedera lizei
Garrya elliptica 'James Roof'
Hedera algeriensis 'Gloire de
Marengo'
H. colchica 'Dentata'
H. c. 'Dentata Variegata'
H. c. 'Sulphur Heart'
(formerly 'Paddy's Pride')
H. helix
H. h. 'Buttercup'
H. h. 'Oro di Bogliasco'
(formerly 'Goldheart')
H. h. 'Parsley Crested'
(formerly 'Cristata')
H. h. 'Pedata'
H. hibernica
Holboellia coriacea
Hydrangea anomala subsp.
petiolaris
Lapageria rosea
Lonicera × italica
L. japonica
L. j. 'Halliana'
L. periclymenum 'Belgica'
L. p. 'Serotina'
L. × purpusii 'Winter Beauty'
Parthenocissus henryana
P. quinquefolia
P. tricuspidata 'Veitchii'
Pileostegia viburnoides
Rosa 'Albéric Barbier'
R. 'Constance Spry'
R. 'Danse du Feu'
R. 'Gloire de Dijon'
R. 'New Dawn'
R. Warm Welcome (also
known as 'Chewizz')
R. 'Zéphirine Drouhin'
Schizophragma hydrangeoides
'Roseum'
Stephanotis floribunda

Coastal areas

Billardiera longiflora
Bougainvillea × buttiana 'Mrs
Butt' (only if you live on
Mediterranean coast!)
Garrya elliptica 'James Roof'
Jasminum nudiflorum
J. officinale
Lonicera × brownii
'Dropmore Scarlet'
L. × italica
L. japonica
L. j. 'Halliana'
L. periclymenum 'Belgica'

L. p. 'Serotina'
Pyracantha rogersiana
P. Saphyr Orange (also
known as 'Cadange')

Drought tolerant

Abutilon megapotamicum
Bougainvillea × *buttiana* 'Mrs
Butt'
Ceanothus 'Italian Skies'
Chaenomeles speciosa
'Geisha Girl'
C. s. 'Moerloosei'
Cotoneaster frigidus
'Cornubia'
C. horizontalis
C. lacteus
Eccremocarpus scaber
Euonymus fortunei 'Emerald
'n' Gold'
E. f. 'Silver Queen'
× *Fatshedera lizei*
Fremontodendron 'California
Glory'
Garrya elliptica 'James Roof'
Hedera algeriensis 'Gloire de
Marengo' (formerly *H.
canariensis*)
H. colchica 'Dentata'
H. c. 'Dentata Variegata'
H. c. 'Sulphur Heart'
(formerly 'Paddy's Pride')
H. helix
H. h. 'Buttercup'
H. h. 'Oro di Bogliasco'
(formerly 'Goldheart')
H. h. 'Parsley Crested'
(formerly 'Cristata')
H. h. 'Pedata'
H. hibernica
Hydrangea anomola subsp.
petiolaris
Jasminum beesianum
J. mesnyi
J. nudiflorum
J. officinale
J. o. 'Clotted Cream'
J. o. Fiona Sunrise (also
known as 'Frojas')
J. polyanthum
Lathyrus latifolius
L. odoratus
Lonicera × *brownii*
'Dropmore Scarlet'
L. × *italica*
L. japonica
L. j. 'Halliana'
L. periclymenum 'Serotina'
L. × *purpusii* 'Winter Beauty'

Parthenocissus henryana
P. quinquefolia
P. tricuspidata 'Veitchii'
Passiflora caerulea
Pyracantha rogersiana
P. Saphyr Orange (also
known as 'Cadange')
Rosa 'Albéric Barbier'
R. 'Albertine'
R. Altissimo
(also known as 'Delmur')
R. 'American Pillar'
R. banksiae 'Lutea'
R. 'Bantry Bay'
R. 'Climbing Cécile
Brünner'
R. 'Climbing Iceberg'
R. 'Crimson Glory
Climbing'
R. 'Constance Spry'
R. 'Danse du Feu'
R. filipes 'Kiftsgate'
R. 'Gloire de Dijon'
R. 'Golden Showers'
R. 'New Dawn'
R. 'Rambling Rector'
R. Warm Welcome (also
known as 'Chewizz')
R. 'Zéphirine Drouhin'
Solanum crispum
S. laxum 'Album' (formerly
S. jasminoides 'Album')
Vitis vinifera 'Purpurea'
Wisteria floribunda 'Multijuga'
(formerly 'Macrobotrys')
W. f. 'Rosea'
W. sinensis
W. s. 'Alba'

Wet, boggy soil

Hedera colchica 'Dentata
Variegata'
H. c. 'Sulphur Heart'
(formerly 'Paddy's Pride')
H. helix
Hydrangea anomala subsp.
petiolaris

Autumn leaf colour

Celastrus orbiculatus
C. scandens
Parthenocissus henryana
P. quinquefolia
P. tricuspidata 'Veitchii'
Vitis amurensis
V. coignetiae
V. vinifera 'Purpurea'
V. v. 'Siegerrebe'

Berries, decorative seed pods/heads and fruits

These plants have the added
benefit of attracting
wildlife into the garden

Actinidia deliciosa
A. kolomikta
Akebia quinata
A. trifoliata
Ampelopsis brevipedunculata
var. *maximowiczii* 'Elegans'
Aristolochia macrophylla
(formerly *A. durior*)
Berberidopsis corallina
Billardiera longiflora
Celastrus orbiculatus
C. scandens
Chaenomeles speciosa
'Geisha Girl'
C. s. 'Moerloosei'
Clematis 'Bill MacKenzie'
C. cirrhosa var. *purpurascens*
'Freckles'
C. c. 'Wisley Cream'
C. flammula
C. 'Frances Rivis'
C. 'Purple Spider'
C. tangutica
C. × *triternata*
'Rubromarginata'
C. vitalba
Cotoneaster frigidus
'Cornubia'
C. horizontalis
C. lacteus
Euonymus fortunei 'Silver
Queen'
Ficus pumila
Fremontodendron 'California
Glory'
Hedera algeriensis 'Gloire de
Marengo' (formerly *H.
canariensis*)
H. colchica 'Dentata'
H. c. 'Dentata Variegata'
H. c. 'Sulphur Heart'
(formerly 'Paddy's Pride')
H. helix
H. h. 'Oro di Bogliasco'
(formerly 'Goldheart')
H. hibernica
Holboellia coriacea
Humulus lupulus 'Aureus'
Jasminum beesianum
J. polyanthum
Lathyrus latifolius
L. odoratus
Lonicera × *italica*

L. japonica
L. j. 'Halliana'
L. periclymenum 'Belgica'
L. p. 'Serotina'
Passiflora caerulea
Pyracantha rogersiana
P. Saphyr Orange (also
known as 'Cadange')
Rosa banksiae 'Lutea'
R. Altissimo (also known as
'Delmur')
R. 'Rambling Rector'
Schisandra rubriflora
Solanum crispum
S. laxum 'Album' (formerly
S. jasminoides 'Album')
Sollya heterophylla
Stauntonia hexaphylla
Stephanotis floribunda
Tropaeolum speciosum
Vitis amurensis
V. coignetiae
V. vinifera 'Purpurea'
V. vinifera 'Siegerrebe'
Wisteria floribunda 'Multijuga'
(formerly 'Macrobotrys')
W. f. 'Rosea'
W. sinensis
W. s. 'Alba'

Red flowers or berries

Abutilon megapotamicum
Asteranthera ovata
Berberidopsis corallina
Celastrus orbiculatus
C. scandens
Clianthus puniceus
Cotoneaster frigidus
'Cornubia'
C. horizontalis
C. lacteus
Eccremocarpus scaber
Jasminum beesianum
Lonicera × *brownii*
'Dropmore Scarlet'
Pyracantha rogersiana
P. Saphyr Orange (also
known as 'Cadange')
Rosa Altissimo (also known
as 'Delmur')
R. 'American Pillar'
R. 'Crimson Glory
Climbing'
R. 'Danse du Feu'
Schisandra rubriflora
Tropaeolum majus 'African
Queen'
T. speciosum

Yellow flowers or berries

Abutilon megapotamicum
Campsis radicans f. flava
Celastrus orbiculatus
Chimonanthus praecox 'Luteus'
Clematis 'Bill MacKenzie'
C. tangutica
Fremontodendron 'California Glory'
Hedera helix 'Buttercup' (if grown in full sun)
Humulus lupulus 'Aureus'
Jasminum mesnyi
J. nudiflorum
Lonicera japonica
Rosa banksiae 'Lutea'
R. 'Gloire de Dijon'
R. 'Golden Showers'
Thunbergia alata

Pink flowers or berries

Bougainvillea x buttiana 'Mrs Butt'
Calystegia hederacea 'Flore Pleno'
Chaenomeles speciosa 'Geisha Girl'
Clematis 'Continuity'
C. 'Elizabeth'
C. 'M. Koster' (formerly 'Margot Koster')
C. montana var. rubens 'Odorata'
C. m. var. r. 'Pink Perfection'
C. m. var. r. 'Tetrarose'
C. 'Nelly Moser'
C. 'Princess Diana'
C. 'Rosea'
C. x triternata 'Rubromarginata'
Euonymus fortunei 'Silver Queen'
Hoya carnosa
Jasminum x stephanense
Lapageria rosea
Lathyrus latifolius
L. odoratus
Lonicera x italica
L. periclymenum 'Belgica'
Rosa 'Albertine'
R. 'Bantry Bay'
R. 'Climbing Cécile Brünner'
R. 'Constance Spry'
R. 'New Dawn'
R. 'Zéphirine Drouhin'
Schisandra rubriflora
Wisteria floribunda 'Rosea'

Orange flowers or berries

Campsis radicans f. flava
Eccremocarpus scaber
Lonicera x brownii 'Dropmore Scarlet'
Passiflora caerulea (orange fruits)
Pyracantha rogersiana
P. Saphyr Orange (also known as 'Cadange')
Rosa Warm Welcome (also known as 'Chewizz')
Thunbergia alata
Tropaeolum majus 'African Queen'

Blue/purple/lilac flowers

Akebia quinata
A. trifoliata
Aristolochia macrophylla (formerly A. durior)
Ceanothus 'Italian Skies'
Clematis cirrhosa var. purpurascens 'Freckles'
C. x durandii
C. 'Frances Rivis'
C. 'Gipsy Queen'
C. 'Helsingborg'
C. 'Purple Spider'
C. 'Royal Velours'
C. tibetana subsp. vernayi 'Glasnevin Dusk'
C. x triternata 'Rubromarginata'
C. 'Velosa Violacea'
Cobaea scandens
Hardenbergia violacea
Holboellia coriacea
Ipomoea tricolor 'Heavenly Blue'
Lathyrus odoratus
Passiflora caerulea
Plumbago auriculata
Solanum crispum
Sollya heterophylla
Stauntonia hexaphylla
Wisteria floribunda 'Multijuga' (formerly 'Macrobotrys')
W. sinensis

Cream/white flowers

Actinidia deliciosa
A. kolomikta
Araujia sericifera
Billardiera longiflora
Celastrus orbiculatus

Chaenomeles speciosa 'Moerloosei'
Clematis 'Apple Blossom'
C. armandii
C. cirrhosa var. balearica
C. c. var. purpurascens 'Freckles'
C. c. 'Wisley Cream'
C. 'Continuity'
C. flammula
C. montana var. grandiflora
C. napaulensis
C. vitalba
Cotoneaster frigidus 'Cornubia'
C. lacteus
Hoya carnosa
Hydrangea anomala subsp. petiolaris
Jasminum officinale
J. o. 'Clotted Cream'
J. o. Fiona Sunrise (also known as 'Frojas')
J. polyanthum
Lonicera x italica
L. japonica 'Halliana' (flowers age to yellow)
L. periclymenum 'Serotina'
L. x purpusii 'Winter Beauty'
Passiflora caerulea
Pileostegia viburnoides
Pyracantha rogersiana
P. Saphyr Orange (also known as 'Cadange')
Rosa 'Albéric Barbier'
R. 'Climbing Iceberg'
R. filipes 'Kiftsgate'
R. 'Rambling Rector'
Schizophragma hydrangeoides 'Roseum'
Solanum laxum 'Album' (formerly S. jasminoides 'Album')
Stauntonia hexaphylla
Stephanotis floribunda
Trachelospermum jasminoides
Wisteria sinensis 'Alba'

Foliage

Actinidia deliciosa
A. kolomikta
Ampelopsis brevipedunculata var. maximowiczii 'Elegans'
Aristolochia macrophylla (formerly A. durior)
Billardiera longiflora
Celastrus orbiculatus
C. scandens

Cotoneaster frigidus 'Cornubia'
C. horizontalis
C. lacteus
Euonymus fortunei 'Emerald 'n' Gold'
E. f. 'Silver Queen'
x Fatshedera lizei
Ficus pumila
Hedera algeriensis 'Gloire de Marengo' (formerly H. canariensis)
H. colchica 'Dentata'
H. c. 'Dentata Variegata'
H. c. 'Sulphur Heart' (formerly 'Paddy's Pride')
H. helix
H. h. 'Buttercup'
H. h. 'Oro di Bogliasco' (formerly 'Goldheart')
H. h. 'Parsley Crested' (formerly 'Cristata')
H. h. 'Pedata'
H. hibernica
Humulus lupulus 'Aureus'
Parthenocissus henryana
P. quinquefolia
P. tricuspidata 'Veitchii'
Pileostegia viburnoides
Pyracantha rogersiana
P. Saphyr Orange (also known as 'Cadange')
Sollya heterophylla
Vitis amurensis
V. coignetiae
V. vinifera 'Purpurea'
V. v. 'Siegerrebe'

Plant index